Making the Most of Today

Making the Most of Today

Daily Readings for Young People on Self-Awareness, Creativity, and Self-Esteem

Pamela Espeland and Rosemary Wallner

Free Spirit
PUBLISHING

Copyright © 1991 by Pamela Espeland

Library of Congress Cataloging-in-Publication Data
Espeland, Pamela, 1951-
     Making the most of today: daily readings for young
    people on self-awareness, creativity, and self-esteem /
    [Pamela Espeland, Rosemary Wallner].
       p. cm.
    Includes index.
    Summary: Daily readings for all young people who
    want to know themselves better, be more creative, and
    feel better about themselves.
    ISBN 0-915793-33-4
    1. Self-perception in adolescence—Juvenile
literature. 2. Creative ability in adolescence—Juvenile
literature. 3. Self-respect in adolescence—Juvenile
literature. [1. Self-perception. 2. Creative ability. 3.
Self-respect. 4. Adolescence.] I. Wallner, Rosemary,
1964-   . II. Title
BF723.S28E86 1991   91-14494
158'.1--dc20   CIP
                                 AC

10 9 8 7 6 5 4
Printed in the United States of America

Cover and book design by MacLean and Tuminelly

Free Spirit Publishing Inc.
400 First Avenue North, Suite 616
Minneapolis, MN 55401
(612) 338-2068

To John and Jonah, with unconditional love
    PLE

To Alan
    RFW

"The true self is always in motion like music, a river of life, changing, moving, failing, suffering, learning, shining."

—Brenda Ueland

"The greatest thing in the world is to know how to be one's own self."

—Michel E. de Montaigne

"When face to face with oneself, there is no cop-out."

—Duke Ellington

Introduction

This is a book of daily readings for all young people who want to know themselves better, be more creative, and feel better about themselves.

It is not specifically for recovering young people, meaning that it is not based on any Twelve Step program or group. But the emphasis on self-awareness and self-esteem is certainly consistent with those programs and groups, so recovering young people should feel welcome here, too.

We hope that young people will read these daily entries on their own—that this will be *your* book. We are recommending it for ages 11 and up, just as a general guideline. This doesn't mean that kids under 11 shouldn't read it if they want to, or that adults should Keep Out. In fact, we often recommend that young people talk with trusted adults about the issues and questions raised in the daily entries. Ideally, this book will be shared within the family.

Parents, teachers, and counselors: If you're giving this book to a young person in your care, consider pairing it with a blank-book journal. Kids may want to record their thoughts, ideas, and personal growth.

January 1

"What you can do, or dream you can, begin it."

—Johann von Goethe

I t's always exciting to start a New Year. Anything can happen. Some people make New Year's resolutions—promises to themselves. Some people list goals they want to achieve. You may want to try this: Write down your dreams for the year. What do you hope will happen? What would you like to do? Put your list away until the end of the year. Then look at it to see how many of your dreams came true.

TODAY

I'll dream of the year ahead.

*"You say you want to 'be somebody'—
then apparently you don't want to be
yourself."*

—Hugh Prather

Do adults always ask you, "What are you going to be when you grow up?" Do they tell you, "Study hard so you'll be somebody?" In fact, you're already somebody. You don't have to wait to see how you'll turn out. Over the years, you'll grow and change. But you'll never be more you than you are right now.

TODAY

I'll appreciate who I am
and where I am in my life.

January 3

> "All acts performed in the world begin in the imagination."
>
> —Barbara Grizzuti Harrison

An Australian basketball team wanted to be able to shoot more baskets. Some team members practiced taking foul shots for 30 minutes every day. Other team members didn't actually shoot baskets. They imagined themselves shooting baskets. They improved almost as much as the group that practiced for 30 minutes every day! Many athletes use their imaginations to become more successful. They picture themselves getting better, and it really happens.

I'll imagine myself getting better at...?

3

January
4

"It's okay if you mess up. You should give yourself a break."

—Billy Joel

Sometimes it's all right to get mad at yourself. When you do something you know you shouldn't, a little anger can set you straight. But don't let it get out of hand. Don't start hating yourself because you make mistakes. Give yourself a break; you're only human. As long as you learn from your mistakes, you're doing okay. Forgive yourself and get on with your life.

TODAY

**I'll forgive myself
for a past mistake.**

4

"Perfection is a perfect bore."
—John-Roger and Peter McWilliams

Imagine, for a moment, a perfect world....What would there be to do? No problems to solve. No causes to believe in. Nobody to help. Luckily, says Barbara Lewis, author of *The Kid's Guide to Social Action*, "the real world is chock-full of real problems to solve...Isn't it exciting for you that all these problems haven't already been solved? Could you think of anything more boring than growing up in a world where everything had already been done?"

TODAY

**I'll think of a problem
I'd like to help solve.**

January 6

"There is a kind of victory in good work, no matter how humble."

—Jack Kemp

Many people think that to be happy in life, you need a high-paying, high-status job. In fact, you can be happy doing anything, as long as you enjoy it and feel right about it. Start now by taking pride in whatever you do. If it's your day to wash the dishes, make them gleam. If you have catbox duty, go for first prize. Get used to feeling proud of your work. That feeling will guide you in the right direction.

TODAY

I'll do good work.

January 7

"You cannot shake hands with a clenched fist."

—Indira Gandhi

You don't have to like everybody. But sometimes you have to deal with people you don't like. There are ways to make this easier on yourself (and them). Hear their opinions. Be careful of their feelings. Treat them with respect. Be willing to compromise. Listen. You may learn that you have more in common than you think.

TODAY

I'll try listening instead of yelling.

7

January 8

"Don't let any person take away your happiness."

—M. Bertha Poupore

Did you know that you can collect and store good feelings? Counselors Gershen Kaufman and Lev Raphael suggest this easy way:

1. Write down five things that happened today which you feel good about.
2. Do this every day—weekdays, weekends, school days, vacation days.
3. Keep your Happiness Lists in a special notebook or folder.
4. Whenever you need a boost, read through your Happiness Lists and enjoy your good feelings all over again.

TODAY

I'll start a Happiness List.

January 9

"My greatest fear is to go through life without any real friends."

—Holly, 17

Friendships don't just happen. They take energy and effort. Start by letting people know that you're interested in them. Don't just talk about yourself. Ask questions about them. Then listen to what they say. (It's amazing how many people forget to do this, or don't know how.) Helen Gurley Brown pointed out, "If you are doing all the talking, you are boring somebody."

TODAY

I'll learn something new about a friend.

January 10

"When you betray somebody else, you also betray yourself."

—Isaac Bashevis Singer

Shauna liked Ben. It was a secret. One day she told Kelly, who promised not to tell anybody else. At lunch, everyone started talking about which girls liked which boys. Shauna was the only one who didn't say anything. Kelly felt powerful—she knew something nobody else knew. She blurted out Shauna's secret. Everyone teased Shauna. Suddenly Kelly didn't feel powerful; she felt terrible. She knew that Shauna would never trust her again.

If someone trusts me with a secret, I'll keep it.

10

January
11

*"Creative minds have always been
known to survive any kind of bad training."*

—Anna Freud

Yusef plays the piano by ear. He can
play almost anything he hears. He is
obviously talented, so his parents start him on
piano lessons. The first thing his teacher tells
him is to stop playing the piano by ear! Some
teachers are good for you. They nourish your
talents and help them grow. Other teachers
aren't so helpful. But nobody can take your
talents away from you. You will still have
them after these teachers have come and gone.

TODAY

I'll enjoy my creative mind.

"To disagree, one doesn't have to be disagreeable."

—Barry Goldwater

Which one would you rather hear?
1. "That's a really stupid idea."
2. "I don't agree with your idea. Here's why...."

The answer should be obvious. Nobody would enjoy hearing #1. People can disagree and still respect each other. They can argue without attacking. They can stick up for themselves without putting each other down. And sometimes they can turn disagreements into agreements, just by being respectful.

TODAY

If I disagree with someone, I'll be polite about it.

12

January 13

"Too many activities, and people, and things. Too many worthy activities, valuable things, and interesting people."

—Anne Morrow Lindbergh

A full and busy life is a mixed blessing. On the one hand, it's great to have tons of wonderful things to do. On the other hand, we can't do everything. We end up not doing anything well. Or we don't have fun doing things we used to enjoy. If your life feels too crowded, it's time to make some choices. What can you cut out? What can you rearrange?

TODAY

**I'll make my life
a little less crowded.**

January 14

"You feel the way you do right now because of the thoughts you are thinking at this moment."

—David D. Burns

How do you feel right now, this second, while you're reading this? Good, bad, happy, sad, blah, scared, frustrated, excited? Your thoughts have the power to change your feelings. And you have the power to change your thoughts. If you don't like what you're thinking, then think about something else. Your feelings will follow.

TODAY

**I am in charge of my thoughts.
I can choose what to think.
I'll choose to think positively.**

January 15

"The Vietnamese are our brothers, the Russians are our brothers, the Chinese are our brothers; and one day we've got to sit down together at the table of brotherhood."

—Dr. Martin Luther King, Jr.

Today is Dr. King's birthday. It's a good day to remember his dream of freedom and understanding for all people. It's a good day to practice peace in your own life. If there's someone you've been arguing with...someone you owe an apology to...someone you've been teasing...why wait until tomorrow?

TODAY

I'll practice peace.

15

January 16

"*Advice is what we ask for when we already know the answer but wish we didn't.*"

—Erica Jong

Think about it: How often do you ask for advice from someone you respect? How often do you listen with an open mind? How often do you take that advice seriously, maybe even act on it? Most of the time, we don't want advice. We want someone to agree with us and tell us we're doing the right thing.

TODAY

I'll ask for advice and really listen.

January 17

"Tell me and I forget, teach me and I remember, involve me and I learn."

—Benjamin Franklin

What are you learning in school? Nothing? Zero? Zip? Then do something about it. Set goals for yourself. Ask questions in class. Find an ally—a teacher who can help you get more out of school. If you want to learn, you will learn. (P.S. Today is Benjamin Franklin's birthday.)

TODAY

I'll think about what I'm getting out of school. How can I play a bigger part in my own learning? Who can I talk to about this?

17

"Umty-tiddly, umty-too."

—Eeyore in *Winnie-the-Pooh* (A.A. Milne)

Adults who want to be more creative are often told, "Think like a kid!" That's because kids have more active imaginations. One good way to think like a kid is by reading children's books. What are some favorites you haven't read for a while? Are they sitting forgotten on a shelf somewhere? Maybe it's time to spark your imagination and meet old friends again. (P.S. Today is A.A. Milne's birthday.)

TODAY

I'll treat myself by re-reading a favorite children's book.

18

January
19

"Which do you want first—the good news, or the bad news?"

—American saying

What's your first feeling when someone asks you this question? Are you afraid of the bad news, or excited about the good news? Most people focus on the negative. It seems bigger and more important than the positive. The same is true of the way we see ourselves. Ellen Goodman reminds us, "The things we hate about ourselves aren't more real than things we like about ourselves." Yet those are what we focus on.

TODAY

I'll focus on my good points.

January 20

*"Tomorrow is often the busiest day
of the year."*

—Proverb

I s procrastination a problem for you? Do
you put off until tomorrow what you could do
today, or should have done yesterday?
Procrastination can raise your stress level and
lower your self-esteem. If you're caught in
this trap, try these tips:

1. Give yourself more time than you think a
   project will take.
2. Don't aim for perfection.
3. Do the hardest part first—then everything
   else will seem easy.
4. Reward yourself after each step.

TODAY

**I'll start a project
I've been putting off.**

January 21

"If your ship doesn't come in, swim out to it!"

—Jonathan Winters

You want many things out of life, and you know you're going to have to work to achieve them. Although it's easier to sit back and wait for opportunities to find you, the best ones come when you pursue them. How can you go after what you really want? Start with a small, reachable goal. Think about how you can reach it. Then do it. Once you've achieved that goal, look for others. No one can stop you now.

I'll make my own opportunities.

January 22

*"I never learned anything talking.
I only learn things when I ask questions."*

—Lou Holtz

Someone once said, "When you do all the talking, you only learn what you already know." If you really want to learn something new, keep your ears open and your mouth closed. Listen to what other people have to say. Pay attention to their ideas. Then ask questions. There are many adults who enjoy the company of curious kids. They will be glad to answer your questions.

TODAY

**I'll ask questions and
learn something new.**

22

January 23

"A human being's first responsibility is to shake hands with himself."

—Henry Winkler

How well do you know yourself? Not just your likes and dislikes, your favorite color or TV program, but the real, inside, whole-person you? What are your talents? What are your interests? What do you believe in? What things are most important to you? What kind of person are you? (If you don't know yourself, how can you expect others to know you and understand you?)

TODAY

**I'll get to know myself
a little better.**

23

January 24

"Everything starts as somebody's daydream."

—Larry Niven

Writer Mary Shelley daydreamed the story of Frankenstein. Thomas Edison once said, "I never created anything, my dreams did." Have you ever "dreamed up" the answer to a question or a problem? Here's how to take a Daydream Trip: Relax. Breathe deeply. Imagine yourself floating off to your favorite place. Smell the smells, see the sights, hear the sounds. Let your thoughts go until they end up someplace interesting.

TODAY

I'll make time to daydream.

January 25

"My training as a painter helped me as a writer."

—Mark Strand

Mark Strand is a poet. In fact, he's America's Poet Laureate. How could knowing about painting help his writing? Think about it. Creative people make connections other people don't. (A Swiss mountain climber named George de Mestral picked burs off his pants and invented Velcro.)

TODAY

I'll keep my eyes (and mind) open
for new connections.

January 26

"When in doubt, tell the truth."

—Mark Twain

Sometimes lying seems easier than telling the truth. But when you tell one lie, you almost always have to make up two or three more. Then you have to remember all of them, in the right order, plus the people you told them to...and suddenly you're trapped. Lies may be easy to tell, but they're difficult to erase.

I'll think first before telling a lie.

January
27

"Habit, if not resisted, soon becomes necessity."

—St. Augustine

Some habits are good for you, like getting enough sleep. Other habits can hurt you. Cigarettes, alcohol, and other drugs are all habit-forming. They can run your life and ruin your health. Stay away from them. Or at least use common sense and learn about them first. Much of what you read and hear will be scary or too simple—like "Just say no." But there are hard facts available on smoking, drinking, and drugs. Get the facts.

I'll take care of my health.

27

January 28

"I've made my contribution to culture, for better or worse."

—Bill Cullen

There are many ways you can "contribute to culture." Maybe you're a talented artist or performer—a poet, painter, actor, singer, or kazoo player. But even if you're sure that you have no special talents, you can still spread some culture around. Have you read a good book lately? Heard an exciting new piece of music? Seen a great movie? Then tell a friend. Pass the word. Share the news.

TODAY

I'll share my talents, or my opinions.

"I'd rather be failing at something I enjoy than be a success at something I hate."

—George Burns

Tom is a terrible singer who loves to sing. He's a football genius who hates playing football. What happens when your talents and feelings disagree? People may pressure you to use a talent you don't enjoy. Or they may tell you to quit something you don't have a talent for. Can you think of ways to bring your talents and feelings together? (Maybe Tom can coach football and sing after practice in the locker room shower.)

TODAY

I'll brainstorm ways to match my talents with my feelings.

January 30

"One kind word can warm three winter months."

—Japanese proverb

It's not always easy to give compliments. Sometimes jealousy can get in the way. If a friend scores high on a test and you don't, it's normal to feel a little green with envy. If your brother wins a contest or your sister brings home a trophy, you may resent their success. Say something nice anyway. Someday you'll deserve a compliment. If you give them freely, others may, too.

TODAY

I'll compliment someone who deserves it.

30

January 31

"When the going gets tough,
I go to Grandma's."

—T-shirt saying

In the cartoon strip, "One Big Happy," two children live very near their grandparents. They see them almost every day. They go shopping together, read stories, take walks, and share meals. Most of us live too far from our grandparents to spend much time with them. If yours are in another town or state, they would probably love getting a letter from you (even a short one). And you'll feel good about writing it.

TODAY

I'll write a letter to my grandparents or someone else I care about.

February
1

"Never give in, never, never, never, never."

—Winston Churchill

You have the right to form your own opinions and beliefs. And you have the right to change your opinions and beliefs as often as you like. Nobody else can tell you what to think. Nobody can force you to believe what you don't want to believe. At the same time, you have the right to keep an open mind. You can ask questions and learn. No one can take these rights away from you.

TODAY

I'll exercise my right to be myself.

February
2

"It's important to be involved and stand up for what you believe in."

—Ione Skye

What's going on in your neighborhood? In your local government? What issues are causing controversy in your community? Too often, it's easy to go to school, do homework, eat, and sleep, all without reading a newspaper or watching the news on TV. Take time to find out about your surroundings and get involved. You'll meet new people as you make a difference in your world.

TODAY

I'll get involved in something outside of school.

33

February 3

"The human mind, once stretched to a new idea, never goes back to its original dimensions."

—Oliver Wendell Holmes

There are many ways to s-t-r-e-t-c-h your mind. One is by trying to see the other side of an argument. Another is by staying open-minded, willing to hear and think about new ideas. Brain-teasers and puzzles are good mind-stretchers. So are books on topics that you don't know much about. What's your favorite way to exercise your brain?

I'll learn something new.

February 4

"If you're going to be able to look back on something and laugh about it, you might as well laugh about it now."

—Marie Osmond

When Jonah was four years old, he rinsed his mom's contact lenses down the sink. Back then, she was angry and he was sorry. Now, eight years later, this is one of their favorite stories. They tell it to their friends and laugh about it together. Over time, even embarrassing events can become funny stories. (When we put them in perspective, we can laugh about them sooner.)

TODAY

I'll tell a funny story from my past.

February
5

"Now, my dears, you may go into the fields or down the lane, but don't go into Mr. McGregor's garden."

—Mrs. Rabbit in *The Tale of Peter Rabbit*
(Beatrix Potter)

Breaking rules is part of being a kid. If someone tells you not to do something, you want to do it even more. Some rules are unfair. But others are meant to keep you safe and out of trouble. If you think a rule is unfair, talk to the people who made it. Try to see their side, too.

I'll talk to an adult about a rule
I think is unfair.

February
6

"There are secrets in all families."

—George Farquhar

Some family secrets should stay "in the family." (For example, your friends don't need to know that your sister snores.) But other family secrets must be told—secrets that make people feel ashamed or afraid. If you have this kind of family secret, tell an adult you trust. If a friend has this kind of family secret, encourage him or her to tell a trusted adult.

TODAY

**I'll think of an adult I can trust.
If I ever need to talk to somebody,
I can go to him or her.**

February
7

"People are really somethin'. They're walking books, all of them. Sometimes you'll only meet them once, but you'll never forget them."

—Cyndi Lauper

Sometimes it's not easy to appreciate the many types of people around you, especially if you don't agree with their opinions or actions. No one said you had to like everyone around you. But even if you don't agree with others, you can still respect them. Respect their opinions and thoughts, just as you'd want them to respect yours.

TODAY

I'll respect other people's actions, beliefs, or opinions, even if I don't agree with them.

February
8

"Beethoven and all those guys had wild thoughts."

—Yo-Yo Ma

Have you ever listened to a symphony by Beethoven? Or looked at a painting by Picasso? Or read a poem by Langston Hughes, Emily Dickinson, Robert Frost, or Gwendolyn Brooks? When you experience the work of an artist, you get a glimpse into his or her "wild thoughts." And you may find yourself having some "wild thoughts" of your own. Many artists turn to other artists for inspiration.

TODAY

I'll appreciate (and maybe create) a work of art.

39

February 9

"Look at yourself every once in a while and point out all the things about yourself that you like. Self-esteem—that's really the most important thing."

—Staci Keanan

"**S**elf-esteem (noun): a confidence and satisfaction in oneself; self-respect." That's a pretty simple definition. Too bad self-esteem isn't as easy to develop as it is to define. But anyone can develop it, including you. One way is by trying something new. If you succeed, great. If you don't, you still had the courage to try. Either way, you build self-esteem.

TODAY

I'll build my self-esteem.

February
10

"An error doesn't become a mistake until you refuse to correct it."

—O.A. Battista

It was bound to happen. You probably saw it coming. Something you did or said has backfired, and now it seems like there's no way out. What can you do to make things right? Apologize? Start over? Ask for help? Sometimes all you can do is stand tall, admit your error, and get on with your life. A lot of times that's all people ask.

TODAY

I'll admit an error.

41

February
11

"I believe foremost in love. I am in love all the time—totally. It's a spiritual, emotional thing."

—k.d. lang

Just hearing the word "love" can make you think of hearts and flowers, hugs and romantic togetherness. But there are so many other kinds of love—love of music and art, love of sports, love of a pet, love of a family member, love of friends, love of country, love of God...the list goes on and on.

I'll think about the many kinds of love in my life.

February
12

"Loneliness and the feeling of being unwanted is the most terrible poverty."

—Mother Teresa

Mother Teresa of Calcutta has spent her life caring for India's loneliest and most unwanted: poor people dying in the streets. She once described herself as "a little pencil in the hand of a writing God who is sending a love letter to the world." In 1979, she was awarded the Nobel Peace Prize. We can't all be Mother Teresas. But we can reach out to people in our own ways.

TODAY

I'll be a friend to someone who needs one.

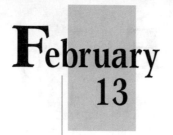

February
13

*"I've finally stopped running away
from myself. Who else is there better to be?"*

—Goldie Hawn

You're you. You can't be anyone else.
But is that really so bad? Take a sheet of
paper and list all the good things about
yourself. (It's okay to use an extra sheet, or
two, or 20.) Write down the names of people
you love and people who love you. Write
down your friends' names, your talents, your
likes, your hopes and dreams. There's a lot to
you. There's a lot to like.

TODAY

I'll be happy with myself.

44

February
14

"Little deeds of kindness, little words of love, help to make earth happy."

—Julia A.F. Carney

Today is St. Valentine's Day. It can be an uncomfortable day for middle school kids. Younger kids can exchange valentines with their whole class. Older kids often have boyfriends or girlfriends. Middle school kids are caught in the middle. But anyone can be a sweetheart today, including you. Do a favor for a friend. Go out of your way to help someone. Show extra kindness.

I'll be a sweetheart.

45

February 15

"No thing is interesting if you're not interested."

—Helen MacInnes

No matter how hard you try, you just aren't interested in your best friend's collection or your neighbor's garden. But that doesn't stop them from talking about their hobbies. They love what they do, and sometimes you find that hard to believe. Be courteous and listen to what they have to say. (No one said you had to join in.)

I'll be tolerant of others.

February
16

"The basis of my music has always been pretty consistent. I've always tried to approach it as a new frontier."

—Stevie Wonder

Creative people don't just create. They also discover. A poet is surprised by her own poem. A painter looks at his painting and sees something brand new. A saxophone player finds a new way to finger a phrase, and it sounds completely different. A dancer learns that she is stronger than she believed. What have you discovered while being creative?

TODAY

I'll surprise myself.

February
17

"I just want to let people know that you can do anything in life. It's out there. You just got to stand up on your feet and do it."

—Bobby Brown

Over and over, people have told you that you can be whatever you want to be. They say that you can do whatever you want to do. But do you believe them? If you don't, it won't matter what they say. You will have set yourself up to fail. Negative thinking does that. (Of course, positive thinking does the opposite.)

TODAY

I'll believe in me.

February
18

"We judge ourselves by what we feel capable of doing, while others judge us by what we have already done."

—Henry Wadsworth Longfellow

One big lie, one bad mistake can ruin a friendship. You know that you're sorry and that you'd never again say or do such a thing. But your friend probably won't feel the same about you for a while (if ever). You'll have to work hard to gain back his or her trust. Maybe you'll succeed; maybe you won't. If the friendship is important to you, keep trying.

TODAY

I'll work to gain back someone's trust.

February 19

> *"I can't wait fifteen years to do my work: Because my ideas are coming now."*
>
> —Sheila Ballantyne

Mary Rodas became vice president of a New York City toy company at age 15. Valerie Tarrant was only 9 when she published her first book. John Clark Hill was 16 when he decided to save a historic building in his home town. Linda Warsaw was 12 when she started Kids Against Crime to help young crime victims. Do you have a great idea?

TODAY

I'll act on one of my ideas, even if it's only a small starting step.

February
20

"I wanted always to appear strong and in control...For many years I was a tough cookie. Then the cookie began to crumble."

—Chris Evert

Do you always have to be The Best? Number One? Superkid? Are you unhappy if you don't have it all—all A's, all the trophies, all the awards, all the prizes, all the praise? You may be a perfectionist. And perfectionism can be a problem. Perfectionists lose their health and their friendships. If you think you may be a perfectionist, tell an adult you trust.

TODAY

I'll find out more about perfectionism.

February
21

"The greatest mistake you can make in this life is to be continually fearing you will make one."

—Elbert Hubbard

Fear is the great paralyzer. Fear of making mistakes keeps us from taking chances, taking risks, and trying new things. It keeps us from learning and growing. Gershen Kaufman and Lev Raphael believe that "every human being has the right to make FOUR BIG MISTAKES every day." What a relief! Not just one mistake, but four! Not little ones, but big ones!

TODAY

I'll exercise my right to make four big mistakes.

52

February
22

"I wasn't lucky. I deserved it."

—Margaret Thatcher

Mrs. Thatcher was Britain's first woman Prime Minister. For more than ten years, she was a powerful world leader. Many successful people, especially girls and women, don't handle their success very well. When others ask them, "How did you get where you are?" they answer, "Oh, I was lucky, I guess." As teacher Barbara Lewis says, "Luck is just another word for work." If you're successful, it's not because you're lucky. It's because you're talented and you work hard.

TODAY

I'll take credit for my success.

February
23

"You can't turn back the clock. But you can wind it up again."

—Bonnie Prudden

Finish this sentence: "If only I hadn't...." Most of us have regrets. In fact, you can't undo things already done. You can't take back words already said. You can't turn back the clock on your life. But you can decide that today will be different. Regret is a waste of time and energy. Leave it behind. As Herbert Prochnow once said, "Our eyes are placed in front because it is more important to look ahead than look back."

TODAY

I won't look back.

February
24

"Don't do nothing halfway, else you find yourself dropping more than can be picked up."

—Louis Armstrong

Do you finish what you start? Or do you begin with a bang and fizzle out at the end? It's hard to do a job or project all the way through. It's easier to come up with excuses like "I don't understand," "I'm bored," or "I don't have enough time." But these are only excuses, and you still have a job to do—only now it will take you longer.

TODAY

I'll finish what I start.

February
25

"Be bold in what you stand for and careful what you fall for."

—Ruth Boorstin

A lot of different people want you to try their product or their way of life, or go along with their beliefs. They may say that "everyone else" is using their product, or "smart people" are living their way, or "good people" are agreeing with their beliefs. How can you know what to do? First, get the facts. Second, take your time to decide. Third, ask people you trust for their opinions and advice. Finally, do what feels right for you.

TODAY

I'll trust my own ability to make good choices.

February
26

"Wherever you go, there you are."

—Buckaroo Banzai

Terell leaves his homework on the bus on purpose. Patti ignores a friend who hurt her feelings. Lauren shuts herself up in her room after an argument with her dad. All three are trying to run away from problems. It doesn't work. Terell still has to do his homework. Patti's feelings are still hurt. Lauren still has to face her dad. Wherever we go, our problems go, too. Wherever we are, there they are.

TODAY

I'll face a problem I've been trying to run away from.

February
27

"As long as you keep a person down, some part of you has to be down there to hold him down, so it means you cannot soar as you otherwise might."

—Marian Anderson

It's easy to pick on people who can't fight back, or make fun of those who are different from us. For a while, this makes us feel powerful and important. But beneath those feelings are others that aren't much fun, like fear and shame. These feelings keep you from being your best.

I won't put anyone down.
If possible, I'll stick up for
someone who needs help.

February 28

"A dream we dream alone is only a dream, but the dream we dream together is reality."

—Yoko Ono

When you can't do something for yourself, what can you do? Ask for help. That sounds simple enough, but many young people won't do it. They stubbornly believe that they have to do everything on their own. They would rather give up a dream than share it. Is there something you dream of doing— something you want to learn or try or accomplish? Why not find a partner?

I'll ask for help if I need it.

February
29

*"Against the assault of laughter,
nothing can stand."*

—Mark Twain

Laughter breaks down barriers between people. It smashes arguments. It cracks smiles. Try attacking your problems with laughter—they will be defenseless. (For some really big laughs, read Mark Twain's famous story, "The Celebrated Jumping Frog of Calaveras County.")

I'll laugh and laugh.
Laughter is joy.
Laughter is healing.
Laughter is good medicine.
Laughter is fun.

March 1

"A lot of people told me I was never going to be anybody. But here I am."

—Rodney A. Grant

Rodney A. Grant is a Native American actor. He played Wind in His Hair in the movie, "Dances with Wolves." For a long time, it looked as if people were right— he never would be anybody. He was born into a troubled family. He had problems with alcohol and the law. He dropped out of high school. Today he's a movie star.

TODAY

**I'll think of all the things I know
I can do and be.**

March 2

> *"Without discipline, there's no life at all."*
>
> —Katharine Hepburn

Is your life a big, confusing mess? Are you constantly forgetting things, losing things, breaking things? Is your room a junkyard? Are you always late? If this sounds familiar, take Florence Kennedy's advice: "Don't agonize. Organize." There are many books, articles, and audio cassettes that can help. Ask your teacher or librarian for ideas. (Even if you're already organized, you could probably be better organized.)

TODAY

**I'll get organized
in one part of my life.**

March 3

"The only people who never fail are those who never try."

—Ilka Chase

Many wise people have written about failure, what it means, and how to cope. Here are four more inspiring sayings:

- Henry Ford: "Failure is the opportunity to begin again more intelligently."
- Max Beerbohm: "Failure is more interesting than success."
- Robert Kennedy: "Only those who dare to fail greatly can ever achieve greatly."
- William D. Brown: "Failure is an event, not a person."

TODAY

I'll make up my own
saying about failure.

63

March 4

"Advice should always be consumed between two thick slices of doubt."

—Walt Schmidt

Just about every day you see something on TV, read something in a book or newspaper, or hear something from another person that doesn't sound quite right. Maybe the facts seem wrong or slanted. When you ask for advice, be prepared for a side order of opinion. Always remember that advice is a suggestion, not a solution.

TODAY

I'll ask for advice. Then I'll solve a problem the way I feel is best.

March 5

*"A little madness in the Spring
Is wholesome even for the King."*

—Emily Dickinson

Every year around this time, millions of kids come down with the same "disease"—spring fever. Maybe you feel like running barefoot through the grass. Or howling at the moon. Or dancing down the street. Or skipping school. These are all perfectly normal feelings. Many adults you know may be having similar feelings. Can you and your family think of something wild and crazy to do together?

TODAY

I'll celebrate the coming of spring.

65

March 6

"'What is the use of a book," thought Alice, "without pictures or conversation?'"

—Alice's Adventures in Wonderland
(Lewis Carroll)

Reading popular novels is easy. Watching TV is easy. So is watching music videos. You don't have to use your imagination; everything is done for you. When you do want to use your imagination, try these tips: Read a poem and picture it in your mind. Turn off the TV. Find a radio station with music you don't usually listen to—classical? jazz? world music?—and imagine scenes to go along with it.

TODAY

I'll exercise my imagination.

March 7

"We get our parents so late in life that it impossible to do anything with them."

—Anonymous

Do you know the saying, "You can't teach an old dog new tricks"? Some parents seem like old dogs. They have their own habits and ideas. They think their way is the only way. In fact, there's a lot that parents can learn from their kids. You see things differently. You have unique thoughts and opinions. What interesting new idea can you share with a parent?

TODAY

I'll tell my parent something he or she doesn't know.

March 8

> *"If you're not feeling good about you, what you're wearing outside doesn't mean a thing."*
>
> —Leontyne Price

Fashions come and go. The in clothes you wore last year are probably out today. And no matter what you wear, you're still you underneath them. You can't pull self-esteem on like a T-shirt. You can't zip up confidence like a pair of jeans. If you're not happy with yourself, no one will notice your clothes. They'll just see an unhappy person.

TODAY

I'll wear my self-esteem for everyone to see.

March

9

"People love chopping wood. In this activity one immediately sees results."

—Albert Einstein

Have you been working too hard? Are you straining your brain? Take a break and do something simple. Pull weeds. Bake cookies. Scrub a sink. Bathe the dog. Straighten out your underwear drawer. You'll give your brain a rest. And you'll have something to show for it.

TODAY

I'll do a task or chore by choice.

March 10

*"Make yourself a blessing to someone.
Your kind smile or pat on the back just
might pull someone back from the edge."*

—Carmelia Elliott

You can probably remember a time when you were feeling blue. Then someone smiled at you for no reason. Or someone said, "You look great today," or "Good work on that report," or "I'm glad we're on the same team." Suddenly you felt better. Smiles and kind words don't cost you anything, but they can make a big difference in another person's day.

TODAY

**I'll do or say something kind,
just because.**

March

11

"The only thing that really matters is what's in the music."

—Terence Trent D'Arby

Y ou say you're a good friend, but do you act like one? You tell people they can trust you, but are you really a trustworthy person? "Action is the only reality," Abbie Hoffman once said, "not only reality, but morality as well." Actions speak louder than words.

TODAY

I'll let my actions speak for me.

March 12

"We are the dreamers of dreams."
—Arthur O'Shaughnessy

Dreams can tell you about yourself. They can help you deal with problems and feelings. But you have to remember them first. Try these tips from author Jonni Kincher:

1. Start a Dream Journal. Keep it next to your bed. Write in it every morning, as soon as you wake up.
2. Keep a glass of water next to your bed. Every night, as soon as you start feeling sleepy, drink the water and tell yourself, "Tonight I will remember my dreams."

TODAY

**I'll write down some dreams
I can remember.**

72

March 13

"We find comfort among those who agree with us—growth among those who don't."

—Frank A. Clark

I t's easy to stick with people you know, habits you're comfortable with, and familiar surroundings. But if you really want to grow as a person, you need new experiences. Listen to classical music if you've never tried it, or rap if you've never tried it. Volunteer at or visit a museum. Eat lunch at an ethnic restaurant (and let the server order for you—be daring). There are possibilities for growth everywhere you look.

TODAY

I'll have a new experience.

March 14

"There's so much in the world to care about."

—Laura Dern

You care about your family and friends. You hope that they will work out their problems, succeed, and feel happy. You help them when they need your help. But there are many more people to care about—the homeless, the poor, disaster victims, the hungry. What can you do for them?

TODAY

I'll look beyond my family and friends to others I can care about and help.

March 15

"Life is like a ten-speed bike. Most of us have gears we never use."

—Charles M. Schulz

Are you using your full potential? That probably sounds like a question a teacher or parent would ask. And if they did, you might shrug or roll your eyes. But what if you asked yourself? How would you answer then? Are there things you'd like to try, but it's easier not to? Think of these as gears you haven't used yet.

TODAY

I'll try something new.

"If you can walk, you can dance.
If you can talk, you can sing."

—A saying from Zimbabwe

Life is full of boring chores and routines. But even the most ordinary actions are transformed when you do them with a joyful touch. If you can get out of bed, you can say "Good morning" to people around you. If you can open your mouth to brush your teeth, you can smile at yourself in the mirror. Even if you have to fake it at first, try it and see what happens.

TODAY

I'll do a boring chore cheerfully.

March 17

"Leave yourself alone."

—Jenny Janacek

Treese doesn't like her hair. Melanie feels too fat. Henry hates his glasses. Robin wishes he got better grades. These kids are always picking on themselves. Maybe they don't say anything out loud. But inside it's pick, pick, pick. What about you? Do you pick on yourself? What would happen if you stopped?

**I'll accept myself,
just the way I am.**

March 18

"Worry often gives a small thing a big shadow."

—Anonymous

Sara lay in bed, her eyes wide open in the dark. Then she heard that noise again...tap, tap against her window. Someone was trying to get in! Her heart raced. She felt too afraid to move. Finally she forced herself to creep to the window. And then she saw the tree branch, blowing in the wind, tapping against the glass. (Many worries disappear when we check them out.)

TODAY

If there's something I'm worried about, I'll check it out. And I'll ask for help if I need it.

"I will tell you what I have learned about myself. For me, a long five- or six-mile walk helps. And one must go alone and every day."

—Brenda Ueland

Writer Brenda Ueland was 94 when she died in 1985. Walking kept her healthy and vigorous all her life. (It also gave her time alone each day, to think and dream.) Is exercise a regular part of your life?

TODAY

I'll feel good about getting enough exercise. Or I'll stop making excuses for why I don't get enough exercise.

March 20

"To escape criticism—do nothing, say nothing, be nothing."

—Elbert Hubbard

Criticism is a fact of life you can't escape. But you can decide to listen or not. Ignore those people who start off, "You always...," "You never...," or "You're a big, ugly...." They aren't trying to help you. They're trying to tear you down. Forget them. But pay attention to people who really care. These are the ones who might say, "I feel this way about..." or "I know you're trying hard, but...."

TODAY

I'll be careful not to criticize people for who and what they are.

March 21

"If all the world's a stage, then let's clean up our act."

—Clinton Hill

Today is Earth Day. What are you doing to save the Earth? Talking about it? Thinking about it? Or taking action? You can save up to nine gallons of water each time you brush your teeth if you don't leave the water running. (Just wet and rinse your toothbrush.) Visit your library for more ideas.

TODAY

I'll do something specific to conserve the Earth's resources.

81

March
22

"One man practicing sportsmanship is far better than 50 preaching it."

—Knute K. Rockne

It's hard to be a good sport, especially when the score was close, the other team had an unfair advantage, or your team deserved to win. But being a good sport shows character and maturity. It shows that you can accept defeat gracefully. You can be a good sport in other places besides the gym or playing field. Celebrate someone else's win, even if it meant your loss.

TODAY

**I'll be a good sport
in all areas of my life.**

March 23

"It does make a difference what you call things."

—Kate Douglas Wiggin

"**S**ticks and stones can break my bones but names can never hurt me...." You probably learned that rhyme as a young child. Don't believe it. Names can hurt a lot. Children who are called "Fatty" or "Stupid" start believing those names are true. Do you ever call yourself names? What kinds of names? Positive or negative? Helpful or hurtful?

I won't call anyone a hurtful name, including myself.

March

24

Tom Seaver: "Yogi, what time is it?"
Yogi Berra: "You mean now?"

Quick, what time is it? To find the answer, did you look at your watch? A clock on the wall? Your clock radio, or the VCR? Counting all the clocks and watches, you probably have an amazing number of timepieces in your house. Try this experiment some weekend with your family: Don't wear watches, and cover the clocks. Turn off all the alarms. Afterward, talk about some of the things that happened. Talk about how you felt.

TODAY

**I'll make time for something I
really want to do.**

"I love you for what you are, but I love you yet more for what you are going to be."

—Carl Sandburg

Parents see their children as bundles of potential. They enjoy watching them learn, grow, and change. They love their children for what they are, and for what they will become. Can you see the potential in your friends? Are they future teachers, athletes, healers, thinkers, inventors? It might be fun to share what you see with them.

TODAY

I'll imagine my friends as adults, just for fun.

"It is such a secret place, the land of tears."

—Antoine de St. Exupéry

Where do you go when you're feeling sad? Is there someplace you can be alone and cry if you want to? We all need to cry sometimes. Even boys. Even grown-up men. Crying is a way to let go of painful feelings. It can be good for you. Charles Dickens once wrote, "Crying opens the lungs, washes the countenance, exercises the eyes, and softens down the temper, so cry away."

TODAY

I'll remember that it's okay to cry.

March 27

"Trust your hunches."

—Joyce Brothers

It sounds good. It looks good. It seems like a good idea. But something about it doesn't feel right. (You could be facing a new relationship or a new experience. A friend could be trying to talk you into something.) You've tried to find out as much as you can. You've dug for the facts. You've thought about it a lot. And you're still not sure....Trust your hunches. Listen to that little voice inside your head.

I'll put off making a big decision unless it feels 100% right to me.

March 28

*"I wish there were windows to my soul,
so that you could see some of my feelings."*

—Artemus Ward

I t's important to be able to name and describe your feelings. Then you can talk about them more clearly. You can get help understanding the ones that seem confusing to you. Gershen Kaufman and Lev Raphael suggest three ways to grow a Feelings Vocabulary:

1. Listen to other people talk about their feelings.
2. Ask for help explaining your feelings.
3. Read about feelings. (Ask a parent, teacher, or librarian to recommend a book.)

TODAY

I'll learn a new feelings word.

March
29

"A friend is a present you give yourself."
—Robert Louis Stevenson

Making friends is hard work. You have to be willing to reach out, to listen, to be honest and accepting. You have to risk being rejected; not everyone will want to be your friend. Still, a life without friends would be no life at all. As poet Edgar Guest once said, "Who would be happy, first must have a friend."

I'll enjoy my friends.

March 30

"Don't bunt. Aim out of the ballpark."
—David Ogilvy

Why put limits on yourself? Why can't you work to change a law? Why can't you run for class president? Why can't you try out for a team or a school play? Only you can tell yourself, "No." Only you can stop yourself from doing whatever you've always wanted to do. Take a chance; stick your neck out. Maybe you'll find that you can do what you once thought was impossible.

I'll believe I can.

March 31

"Progress involves risk. You can't steal second base and keep your foot on first."

—Frederick Wilcox

You can't get anywhere if you don't take risks. But taking risks is scary. What to do? Try these risk-taking tips from Earl Hipp:

1. Start small. Break your risk into little steps.
2. Give yourself permission to be average or worse.
3. Get support. Find four or five people who will help and encourage you.
4. Celebrate yourself. Rejoice at any success, no matter how small it may seem.

TODAY

I'll practice taking risks.

April 1

"I take care of me. I am the only one I've got."

—Groucho Marx

What have you done for yourself lately? Authors Gershen Kaufman and Lev Raphael spell out six good things to do for yourself. Here are three:

1. Choose something to do just for fun. Then do it whenever you can.
2. Give yourself a present every day. (This doesn't have to cost money. Listen to a favorite tape, or take a bubble bath.)
3. Forgive yourself for something you did in the past.

I'll do one of these good things for myself.

92

"Love yourself first and everything else falls in line."

—Lucille Ball

Here are three more good things to do for yourself from Gershen Kaufman and Lev Raphael:

4. Do at least one thing every day that's good for your body.
5. Do at least one thing every day that's good for your brain.
6. Find an adult you can trust and talk to.

(Tip: Make a list of all six good things—yesterday's and today's—and put it where you can see it every morning.)

I'll do another good thing for myself.

April
3

"When you have to cope with a lot of problems, you're either going to sink or you're going to swim."

—Tom Cruise

Some questions have either a right or a wrong answer. Should I go to school? Should I finish my homework? Should I drink alcohol or smoke cigarettes? You know the right answers to questions like these. The wrong answers can cause problems for you. If you're already carrying more than your share of problems, don't make things worse for yourself. If you need support or encouragement, tell an adult you trust.

TODAY

I won't cause new problems for myself.

April 4

"You never know when you're making a memory."

—Rickie Lee Jones

A song, the sound of a person's voice, a color, a smell—any of these can trigger a memory. Your mind stores an amazing number of memories, from the smallest to the largest life events: a birthday party, a kind word, a graduation ceremony, a hug from a friend, bread baking in the oven, a kiss....And you never know when a memory will pop into your head. What you do today will be tomorrow's memories for you (and maybe someone else).

TODAY

I'll spend time with my memories.

April 5

"Don't believe that winning is really everything. It's more important to stand for something. If you don't stand for something, what do you win?"

—Lane Kirkland

A soccer player becomes a big star. Millions of young people look up to him. He is their hero. One day, he is arrested for drunk driving. Then he is arrested for punching a photographer. Then he divorces his wife. He is still a great soccer player. But his fans are confused. Is he really a hero?

TODAY

I'll decide if my heroes deserve my respect.

April 6

"Think for yourself and let others enjoy the right to do the same."

—Voltaire

Just because you think a certain way about something doesn't mean everybody should. Many people never understand this. They spend their lives trying to get others to agree with them. This leads to arguments, injustices, even wars. You have the right to think for yourself. Respect that right in others, too.

TODAY

I won't try to convince someone else to see things my way.

April 7

"Pain nourishes courage. You can't be brave if you've only had wonderful things happen to you."

—Mary Tyler Moore

I t's hard to believe that anything good can come out of a painful incident. But hard times can test your courage, determination, and strength. You suddenly realize that you can handle it. Afterward, you can say to yourself, "I've survived—I can face just about anything now." The hurt you feel will someday go away. And you'll be stronger.

TODGY

I'll accept that pain is a part of growing up.

"When we ask for advice, we are usually looking for an accomplice."

—Marquis de la Grange

Picture two world leaders, each with a group of advisers. The first leader's advisers are a lot like him. They have similar backgrounds and ideas. They tend to agree with their leader. The second leader's advisers are a mixed group. Some have very different backgrounds and ideas. At least one of them always disagrees with her. Which leader do you think gets the best advice?

TODAY

If I need advice, I'll ask someone I usually don't ask—someone who will probably surprise me.

April
9

"I eat my peas with honey,
I've done it all my life,
It makes the peas taste funny,
But it keeps them on the knife."

—Anonymous

This isn't just a silly rhyme. It's a creative solution to a pea-eating problem. Do you have a problem that needs solving? Brainstorm wild and crazy ideas. Write everything down. Keep writing for five or ten minutes. You'll be amazed at what you come up with. (Can you list 20 more ways to eat peas?)

TODAY

I'll brainstorm solutions for a problem I haven't been able to solve.

April 10

"The way you overcome shyness is to become so wrapped up in something that you forget to be afraid."

—Lady Bird Johnson

Everyone feels shy sometimes. Everyone deals with shyness in his or her own way. Some people pull back into their shells. Others force themselves to reach out. One technique for overcoming shyness is to follow your interests. If you enjoy collecting rubber stamps of Looney Tunes characters, maybe someone else does, too. You two would have a lot to talk about. How could you find out about other collectors?

TODAY

I'll reach out.

April
11

"Only the wearer knows where the shoe pinches."

—American proverb

Has someone ever criticized you? (Unless you're a hermit, the answer is probably "Yes.") Maybe someone told you that your hair was messy or your clothes were wrinkled. Was your first reaction to say, "Mind your own business"? Then you know how it feels to be criticized. The next time you're about to criticize someone else, remember that feeling. If that person wants to improve, so be it. Meanwhile, focus on improving yourself.

TODAY

I won't criticize anyone.

102

"A little rebellion is a good thing."

—Thomas Jefferson

Young people are natural rebels. Pushing limits, breaking rules, and challenging those in authority are all a normal part of growing up. But some young people rebel against everything. They are always pushing and challenging. This makes adults tired, angry, and unwilling to listen. Here's good advice from Jonathan Kozol: "Pick battles big enough to matter, small enough to win."

TODAY

I'll decide which of my "battles" are really worth fighting. I'll try to let the others go.

103

April 13

"Imagination is more important than knowledge."

—Albert Einstein

There's no limit to what your imagination can do. Your unconscious mind holds countless images and ideas. How can you bring them into your conscious mind? Sometimes the best way is...not to try. Take a walk, take a bath, read a book, or listen to music. Just relax. Let the ideas float up....Aha! There's the answer to that science problem you couldn't solve....There's a new way to organize your room....That's how to improve your pitching....(Get the picture?)

TODAY

I'll let my imagination run free.

April 14

"If art doesn't make us better, then what on earth is it for?"

—Alice Walker

People will try to tell you what to think about art. They will give you their opinions of "good art" and "bad art." You can learn from some of these people. But only you can decide what a painting, poem, or piece of music means to you. Does it add something to your life? Does it change the way you experience the world? Does it make you better?

TODAY

I'll hang a new poster or picture in my room.

April
15

"Most problems precisely defined are already partially solved."

—Harry Lorayne

Do you have a problem? Just realizing it is the first step toward solving it. Have you defined your problem—have you spelled it out, written it down, or told somebody about it? Then you've taken the second step. Have you looked at your problem from all sides? That's the third step. Once you can clearly see your problem, you can start making choices about it. And you may find that you've already done the hard part.

TODAY

If I have a problem, I'll define it before trying to solve it.

April 16

"At the touch of love, everyone becomes a poet."

—Plato

He walks by and your heart beats faster....She looks at you and your face turns red....Suddenly you can't think of anything but HIM or HER. You could write a poem, a song, a whole book about his or her wonderful looks, voice, talents, brains. You must be—in love! When you're young (and even when you're old), these feelings can be confusing. They can be overwhelming. They can be exhausting. But they are all perfectly normal.

TODAY

I won't judge my feelings.

April 17

"The safest way to double your money is to fold it over once and put it in your pocket."

—Kin Hubbard

What's one of the biggest problems among kids today? Believe it or not, gambling. More and more young people are betting on everything from sporting events to test scores. It's fun to think you'll be the lucky one—the big winner. Fun but unrealistic. For some people, gambling becomes an addiction, like alcohol or other drugs. If you feel that gambling is hurting you or someone you care about, tell an adult you trust. Get help.

TODAY

I'll think about how I use my money.

April
18

"You are a child of the Universe...you have a right to be here."

—Desiderata

Do you know your basic rights as a human being? Here are four important ones:

- You have the right to make decisions about your life.
- You have the right to say "no" to the demands of others.
- You have the right to respond to people who criticize you or put you down.
- You have the right to share your feelings.

TODAY

I'll exercise one (or more) of my basic rights.

April 19

"Seven days without laughter makes one weak."

—Dr. Joel Goodman

Y ou've heard of rock collections, stamp collections, baseball card collections, and more. But have you ever heard of a humor collection? If you started one, what kinds of things would be in it? Cartoon books, humor tapes, Marx Brothers movies, clown noses, rubber chickens, whoopee cushions? It would be great to have a humor collection. Whenever you needed a good laugh, you'd know where to find one.

TODAY

I'll start a humor collection.

"When you aim for perfection, you discover it's a moving target."

—George Fisher

What's your idea of perfection? Getting the best grades? Being the most popular? Winning the most awards? Excelling at everything you do? Perfectionism is too much pressure to put on yourself. The fact is, nobody's perfect, because perfection is impossible. And if you try to do everything perfectly, you won't do anything well. If you're a perfectionist, don't expect to change overnight. As Colette Dowling says, "Becoming less perfect takes practice."

I'll ease up on myself.

111

April
21

"Make no judgments where you have no compassion."

—Anne McCaffrey

What kinds of things are important to you and your friends—your group? Does it matter what people wear, what music they listen to, how they act, what they believe? What happens when someone doesn't fit your picture or follow your rules? Sometimes groups can be cruel to outsiders. They can be quick to gossip, judge, and criticize. Does this sound like your group?

TODAY

I won't judge others.

112

April 22

"When I'm pushing myself, testing myself, that's when I'm happiest. It's a great reward system."

—Sissy Spacek

How do you motivate yourself? How do you get yourself to do something you really don't want to do? Some people just enjoy the challenge. Others need to reward themselves. They might choose an extra half-hour of TV, or a bowl of ice cream with chocolate sauce. You can probably come up with better ideas. What about walking around the block? Talking on the phone with a friend? Playing a game with your family?

TODAY

**I'll think of healthy ways
to reward myself.**

April 23

"I have always regarded myself as the pillar in my life."

—Meryl Streep

Who can you count on 24 hours a day? Who is always there for you, no matter what? Who knows you better than anyone else? The answer is...you. You can be your own best friend, your own best guide and adviser. You're a strong, capable person, and you can succeed at whatever you choose to do.

TODAY

I'll look inside for strength and encouragement.

April 24

"Delay is the deadliest form of denial."
—C. Northcote Parkinson

At one time or another, you have to do something unpleasant, inconvenient, or hard. Your research paper is due in three weeks...you need to talk with a friend about something serious...your room is a total mess....Life is full of times like these. You can ignore them. You can pretend they don't exist. You can put off doing something about them. But that won't make them go away.

TODAY

I'll accept a responsibility
instead of putting it off.

April
25

"Happiness is having a large, loving, caring, close-knit family in another city."

—George Burns

Does your family get on your nerves? Do you look forward to being on your own someday? If you answered "Yes" to these questions, that's normal. Yet everyone, deep down inside, has a real need for family. We may like our families or not. They may be emotionally healthy or totally goofed up. Yet they give us a sense of belonging, of not being alone in the world. And in most cases, they really do care.

TODAY

I'll be more tolerant of my family.

April 26

"You can't look at a sleeping cat and be tense."

—Jane Pauley

It's easy to get so caught up in school work, friends, and extra activities that you forget to sit back and relax. These things are important, but so are you. Take time today to just be lazy. Listen to your favorite record, read a book or magazine, or watch a sleeping cat. (Z-z-z-z-z-z-z.)

I'll relax.

April
27

*"We don't make mistakes. We just
have learnings."*

—Anne Wilson Schaef

Thomas Edison tried 1,500 different
filaments for the light bulb before finding the
right one. After the last experiment, an
assistant asked, "Well, Mr. Edison, how do
you feel about having 1,500 failures to your
credit?" Edison replied, "No, they weren't
failures. We now know 1,500 light bulb
filaments that don't work."

TODAY

**I'll look for the learning
in a mistake.**

April
28

"Everybody is talented, original, and has something original to say."

—Brenda Ueland

What are your talents? Do you know that you can have many different types? Here are some of the more commonly known types:

1. Intellectual talent (all-around brains).
2. Specific academic talent (smarts in a particular area, like math or science).
3. Creativity (and imagination—your brain knows no limits).
4. Leadership talent (can you convince anyone to do almost anything?).
5. Artistic talent (dancing, singing, drawing, music).

TODAY

I'll recognize my talents.

April
29

*"It is better to know some of the
questions than all of the answers."*

—James Thurber

Sometimes it's hard to admit that you don't know all the answers. Especially when there's someone you want to impress, or when you're feeling shy or afraid of being laughed at. But asking questions isn't a sign of weakness, it's a sign of strength. It shows other people that you're interested in them and what they have to say. It shows them that you're confident enough to take a chance. And you almost always learn something new.

TODAY

I'll ask a question.

April 30

"Those who look for reasons to hate miss opportunities to love."

—Carmen Sylva

There will always be people you can't get along with. You won't like them, and they won't like you. They may even hate you. What can you do? Hating someone back takes a lot of energy. You can try being friendly and see what happens. Maybe things will change; maybe they won't. What's important to remember is that you can't change or control another person's feelings.

TODAY

I'll risk reaching out to someone who doesn't like me.

May 1

"Work for what you truly believe is right. But most of all, do not let anything or anyone tell you that the possible is impossible. For even though we're children, we are the leaders of our future."

—April Chacon

April Chacon was in the seventh grade when she wrote those words. She was part of a group of kids who helped clean up a hazardous waste site, plant hundreds of trees, and more. At first, many people told them these things were "impossible." But April and her friends didn't listen.

TODAY

I'll work for something I believe in.

May 2

"You never really leave who you are."

—Michelle Pfeiffer

Other people may want you to behave in certain ways and believe in certain things. They may have big plans for you. But no matter what they say, you're always you. You have your own personality, tastes, abilities, talents, likes, and dislikes. You know what you stand for and what you can't stand. You know who you are.

I'll be happy being myself.

May 3

"George promised to be good. But it is easy for little monkeys to forget."

—*Curious George* (H.A. Rey)

You promised to clean up your room before bedtime. But you started working on a puzzle, and you forgot. Or you promised to walk the dog. But a friend called you on the phone, and you forgot. Everyone forgets things. Apologize if you need to, and finish the job you promised to do. Then forgive yourself. This gives you practice in forgiving others.

TODAY

If I mess up, make a mistake, or forget something, I'll forgive myself.

May 4

"Why turn a perfectly good frog into a prince?"

—Pogo of *Pogo* (Walt Kelly)

"I'd like Lisa more if she...." "I'd be Michael's friend if he...." Do you sometimes wish you could change your friends? How would you change them? What would you change them into? For fun, think of three things you would change about your best friend. Now picture your friend after those changes. Would he or she still be the same person? Would you still want to be friends?

TODAY

I'll appreciate my friends, just the way they are.

May 5

*"I don't wanna be self-righteous.
I never profess to be a perfect person
because I'm not."*

—M. C. Hammer

You know that nobody's perfect. But some people would like you to think that they are. Maybe they point out your flaws to make themselves look better. Maybe they stress their achievements and make fun of your mistakes. You can draw your own conclusions about people like these. And you can decide not to pay attention to them.

TODAY

I'll be suspicious of anyone who claims to be perfect.

126

"Music has been my playmate...and my crying towel."

—Buffy Sainte-Marie

Music is magic. It can make you feel happy or sad, lonely or glad. It can wake up memories from long ago. It can make you want to dance, sing, or drum on a trash can. You can use music to change your feelings. If you're blue, play cheerful tunes. If you're stressed out, try soft sounds. Experiment with different styles to see what they do to your moods.

TODAY

I'll try listening to
a new kind of music.

127

May 7

"Don't grow up too fast. You only get one shot at being a kid, and you'll be grown up for 80 percent of your life. Why rush it?"

—Chad Gervich

Someone once said, "Youth is wasted on the young." When we're not grown-up, we wish we were. We dream of all the things we'll be able to do when we're adults. We can't wait. It's a switch to meet someone like Chad, 16, who enjoys being and acting his age.

TODAY

I'll enjoy being a kid.

May 8

"Do not make yourself low. People will step on your head."

—Yiddish proverb

In the commercial, the beautiful woman looks into the camera and tells us that she uses a certain brand of hair color "because I'm worth it!" What are you worth? Are you worth treating yourself with respect? Are you worth taking care of your body, your brain, and your reputation? It matters who your friends are. It matters how you act and talk. It matters if you hold your head up high. (That also makes it harder to step on.)

TODAY

**I'll treat myself with respect.
I'm worth it.**

May

9

"You only get out of life what you put into it."

—Ethel Merman

Is your life not going the way you planned? Do you feel like you're stuck in a rut? Are things out of control? Don't just sit there feeling sorry for yourself. Do something. Welcome change. Be willing to toss out old plans and make new ones. Set goals for yourself, then work to achieve them. If there's nothing happening in your life, make something happen. The possibilities are endless if you keep an open mind.

TODAY

I'll get more out of life.

May 10

"Alligator pie, alligator pie,
If I don't get some I think I'm gonna die."

—Dennis Lee

Have you ever wanted something so badly that you thought you couldn't live without it? You talked about it, dreamed about it, planned for it, saved for it, begged for it. Then you either got it or you didn't. If you got it, is it still so important to you? If you didn't, are you still alive?

I'll put my wants in perspective.

May 11

*"You can choose how to handle what
life hands you. You can choose how you
will face life's problems."*

—Gershen Kaufman and Lev Raphael

What would you do if you found a
wallet with $1,000 in it? If you saw your best
friend cheating? If a neighbor offered you
drugs? Life is full of choices, though most
aren't as serious as these. If you aren't sure
how you would handle serious choices, get
practice. Ask an adult to role-play some
with you.

**I'll talk with someone I trust
about a serious choice in my life.**

132

May 12

"I'm not opinionated. I'm just always right."

—T-shirt saying

On a shirt, this saying is funny. But in real life, people who believe they're always right aren't much fun to be around. And they don't have many friends. Maybe it's because friends listen to each other and learn from each other. Maybe it's because friends are willing to admit when they're wrong. Do you know someone who's always right? What's your opinion of him or her?

TODAY

I'll make an extra effort to listen to other people.

May
13

"Mistakes are the portals of discovery."

—James Joyce

Many discoveries have been the result of mistakes or accidents: X-rays, rubber, floating soap, Silly Putty, Slinky toys, Popsicles, and Post-It notes, to name a few. (Did you know that Columbus was originally looking for India?) A mistake can lead you in an exciting new direction, if you're willing to go.

TODAY

I'll let a mistake inspire me, not stop me.

May 14

"Be able to be alone."

—Sir Thomas Browne

Being alone and being lonely are two different things. But some young people can't tell them apart. If they're not with their friends or on the phone, they feel anxious or afraid. So they fill their time with school, sports, work, fun, and busy-ness. And they never get to know themselves. Being alone gives you a chance to think your own thoughts, explore your own interests, dream your own dreams. Try it and you'll find that you're worth getting to know.

I'll spend time with myself.

May

15

"I could tell it was going to be a terrible, horrible, no good, very bad day."

—*Alexander and the Terrible, Horrible, No Good, Very Bad Day*
(Judith Viorst)

Some days are like that. You forget your lunch. You miss the bus. You drop your backpack in the hall and it rips and your colored pencils fall out and tumble down the stairs and people step on them and squash them. You spill chocolate milk down your shirt. Back home, the cat digs her claws into your leg. And...life goes on.

TODAY

I'll remind myself that everybody has bad days—and tomorrow always comes.

May
16

"Once I start filming, I let everything go. I try to forget everything I've done and be as simple as possible. In simplicity there is truth."

—River Phoenix

Do you have a job to do or a problem to solve? K-I-S-S it—Keep It Short and Simple. Don't complicate it with extra information, worry, steps, or stress. Don't ask other people for help unless you really need it. And once you've gotten your job or problem down to the basics, what about yourself? Dag Hammarskjöld was United Nations Secretary General when he wished, "If only I may grow firmer, simpler, quieter, warmer."

TODAY

I'll simplify, simplify.

May 17

"It's very difficult to feel secure."

—Helena Bonham Carter

With all the changes in your life and the world around you, it's tough to feel safe and secure. It seems you're always unsure about something, from trivial things like what to wear, to important things like what to do about your future. Does it help to know that everyone else feels the same way sometimes? No one has all the answers. We all go through periods of feeling unsafe, insecure, unloved, lonely, and miserable. These feelings pass. You, too, will learn to find your security within yourself.

TODAY

I'll remember that everyone feels insecure sometimes.

May 18

"If we bestow a gift or a favor and expect a return for it, it is not a gift but a trade."

—Anonymous

Y ou give your friend a $10 tape and he gives you a $5 puzzle. Do you feel cheated? Yesterday you helped your friend with homework, but today she won't loan you her new jacket. Do you get mad? Giving can be fun and rewarding, unless you always expect something in return.

TODAY

I'll do a favor with no strings attached.

May 19

"The man who has no imagination has no wings."

—Muhammad Ali

Your imagination is good for much more than making up stories. For example, you can use it to solve a problem. Think of all the different choices you have. Close your eyes and imagine yourself choosing each one in turn. Now imagine the consequences, good and bad. Imagine how your family and friends will react. Imagine your future, based on each choice.

TODAY

I'll use my imagination.

May 20

"That's the risk you take if you change: that the people you've been involved with won't like the new you. But other people who do will come along."

—Lisa Alther

Friends grow apart. Interests change. Priorities change. Likes and dislikes change. And sometimes you change faster than your friends. You may mature more quickly. You may move up a grade in school. You may get a job or start a new activity. Or you may go off in a completely different direction, where your friends don't want to follow. Be patient. New friends will come along.

TODAY

I won't be afraid to change.

May
21

*"You have brains in your head. You
have feet in your shoes. You can steer
yourself any direction you choose."*

—*Oh, The Places You'll Go*
(Theodor Seuss Geisel, "Dr. Seuss")

Because you're officially "still a kid,"
there are adults who can tell you what to do.
And you usually have to do what they say.
But they can't decide the course of your life.
They can't decide what kind of person you
will become. They can't tell you what to
believe. All of these things (and more) are
up to you.

TODAY

**I'll think about the direction my
life is taking.**

142

May

22

"Since the beginning each generation has fought nature. Now, in the life-span of a single generation, we must turn around 180 degrees and become the protector of nature."

—Jacques Cousteau

Newspapers, radio broadcasts, and news programs report daily on the problems facing our environment. The outlook is grim, but it's not hopeless yet. The more we learn about what harms the environment, the more we can do help it. Slowly but surely, we're working to save the Earth. What can you do personally?

I'll think of something I can do to help the environment.

143

"What is now proved was once only imagined."

—William Blake

Have you ever had an idea that was strongly criticized? Maybe people called it "impractical" or "impossible." This can hurt, especially if it seems that your idea didn't get a fair chance. But instead of giving up, think positively. How can you use the criticism to strengthen your idea? Can you change your idea to make it more acceptable? Work out some possibilities in your head or on paper. Then take the idea back to your critics and see what they think.

TODAY

**I'll accept constructive criticism
and use it to help myself.**

May 24

"Talk low, talk slow, and don't say too much."

—John Wayne

You blew it. You had a party when your parents were out of town. Or you came home three hours after your curfew (and meanwhile they were worried sick). Or you borrowed a friend's computer game and sat on the disk. This is no time to go on the offensive. Resist the temptation to attack. Admit your mistake. Ask how you can make it up. Most of all, listen. In cases like these, other people have the right to complain.

I'll face a mistake.

May

25

"Always tell the truth—it's the easiest thing to remember."

—David Mamet

From "the dog ate my homework" (when he didn't) to "I like your new haircut" (when we don't), most of us are skilled at lies and fibs. Some we tell to get out of trouble. Others we tell because they're more polite than the truth. And others we tell out of habit; it seems easier than being honest. But even little white lies can turn into a blinding blizzard. Are you a truthful person, or is this something you need to work on?

TODAY

I'll give an honest answer to an uncomfortable question.

May 26

"Laughter is by definition healthy."

—Doris Lessing

Laughter is good for your body. When you laugh, your heart rate increases, which helps your circulation. Your body pumps out hormones that make you more alert. Your lungs stretch and air out. More oxygen goes to your brain. Your skeletal muscles loosen and relax. Your digestive system works better. And those are just the physical benefits. To find out about the mental benefits, see page 237.

TODAY

**I'll do my body a favor
by laughing.**

May 27

"Money is a good servant but a bad master."

—French proverb

Money is probably very important to you. (It is to most people.) You may even have a job to earn money. For some young people, this is a must; they support themselves or help to support their families. But other young people work for money to spend on things they want—clothes, shoes, music, video games. If you're in the second group, think about it. Is your job taking away from your school work, study time, and free time? Is it worth it?

TODAY

I'll put money in perspective.

"A person who aims at nothing is sure to hit it."

—Anonymous

Jennifer decided to start an exercise program. She promised herself that she would do 100 sit-ups a day. She quit after only two days. We all need goals; they give meaning to our lives. But when we set unrealistic goals, we set ourselves up to fail. Instead, choose goals you really believe you can reach. Break them into smaller steps, and forgive yourself if you stumble over a step or two.

I'll review my personal goals. Are they realistic?

May 29

"I think what is happening to me is so wonderful, and not only what can be seen on my body, but all that is taking place inside."

—Anne Frank

How do you feel about your body? Do you like it? Hate it? People with a bad body image often have low self-esteem. They may have eating problems. They often feel embarrassed and sad. If you have a bad body image, tell an adult you trust. Get help so your body image doesn't get in your way.

TODAY

I'll talk about my body image with a trusted friend.

150

May 30

"The worst pains in the world are not physical."

—Don Johnson

I f you fall and bruise yourself, or if you touch a hot pan and burn yourself, those injuries to your body will heal quickly. But if someone makes fun of you, lets you down, or refuses to like you, those injuries to your self-esteem will take longer to heal. Someday they won't hurt as much; someday you'll be able to face that person again. For now, if you're hurting inside, acknowledge your pain. Know that it will pass in time.

TODAY

I'll give myself time to heal.

May

31

"Painting is easy when you don't know how, but very difficult when you do."

—Edgar Degas

When you're a child, it's easy to be creative. You do what comes naturally. You paint what you see in your head. You make up your own songs and dances. Then you start school, and things change. Now there are rules for being creative. There are right ways and wrong ways to paint, sing, and dance. Being creative is hard. (How can you think like a kid again?)

TODO

I'll think like a kid.

June 1

"If you think you can, you can. And if you think you can't, you're right."

—Mary Kay Ash

You've heard of the power of positive thinking. Negative thinking is powerful, too. It can drain your brain, crush your creativity, and sap your strength, mental and physical. It can convince you that you're incapable. In tackling any project or solving any problem, believing in yourself is half the battle. Has negative thinking ever blocked you from reaching a goal or realizing a dream?

TODAY

I'll practice positive thinking.

153

June
2

"Discoveries are often made by not following instructions, by going off the main road, by trying the untried."

—Frank Tyger

It's hard to stick up for what you believe is right. Especially if people around you disagree with you, including your parents and teachers. But if you know you're right, and if you stick to your convictions, you can go far. And you'll eventually meet others who feel the way you do.

TODAY

I'll be my own person.

June 3

"I'd rather be myself than anyone else."

—Shirley MacLaine

Is this saying true for you? Why or why not? What can you do for yourself—what can you change in your life—that will make you want to say this? Maybe it's time to break a bad habit and start a healthier one. Maybe it's time to make some choices, set some goals, plan a direction for yourself. Maybe you just need to smile more often. (Don't laugh. Smiling can help.) What makes you happy? What makes you glad you're you?

I'll be glad I'm me.

June 4

"If you want something very badly, you can achieve it. It may take patience, very hard work, a real struggle, and a long time, but it can be done."

—Margo Jones

What do you really want? What's your biggest, most important goal in life (so far)? What are you doing about it? If it seems too hard or too far away, this Chinese proverb may help you keep things in perspective: "The man who removed the mountain began by carrying away small stones."

I'll do something, small or large, to bring me closer to a personal goal.

June
5

"How do you like to go up in a swing,
Up in the air so blue?"

—Robert Louis Stevenson

When was the last time you went up in a swing? A big one where you could really go high, with the wind streaming through your hair? Maybe you think you're too old for swings. Wrong! Play frees your imagination at any age. (Would you like to go swinging? Take a younger child with you. He or she can be your excuse.)

I'll make time to play.

157

June
6

*"Rest is not a matter of doing
absolutely nothing. Rest is repair."*

—Daniel W. Josselyn

Are you feeling stressed? Then give
yourself a break. Sit down or lie down in a
quiet, private place for ten minutes or an
hour. "Doing nothing" gives your mind and
body a chance to recover. If you can't relax,
try meditating. Breathe in slowly through
your nose and silently count "one." Then
breathe out slowly through your nose and
silently count "two." Focus on your breathing
and counting. Ignore other thoughts and
worries. Quit when you're ready.

TODAY

I'll make time to rest.

June 7

"Life is all memory except for the one present moment that goes by so quickly you can hardly catch it going."

—Tennessee Williams

Has anyone ever told you, "You've got your whole life ahead of you"? In fact, your whole life (so far) is behind you. Except for this moment...right now...which has already passed by the time you reach the end of this sentence. It's good to think about the future, but it's important to live in the present. Dream about tomorrow, but be today.

TODAY

I'll take a moment to experience the moment.

June 8

"There will always be people who appear to be handsomer, prettier, richer, luckier, and better-educated than you. What's the point of comparing? We are all created equal. We are all created to serve in a special way."

—Sol Gordon

There are so many ways to serve—to make a difference in the world and the lives of other people. To find your special way, think of ways you are special. What are your gifts, talents, abilities, and skills? How can you use them to serve?

TODAY

I'll reach out and help someone.

June 9

"The secret of a happy life is to accept change gracefully."

—James Stewart

Y ou can't change change, and you can't make things stay the same. So what can you do? You can accept change, even celebrate it. This is a lot healthier than whining and sulking because things are going to be different. Earnie Larsen says, "There is pain in staying the same, and there's pain in change. Pick the one that moves you forward."

TODAY

I'll accept change.

June 10

"What does it mean to respect life?"

—Steve Darden

When Kyle finds a spider indoors, he catches it and carries it outside. Mae shows her respect for life by taking good care of her cat. Rico is a vegetarian by choice. Steve Darden, a Navajo, goes on to say, "I've grown to understand that life is in everything; every substance has life." He respects all life. What about you? What do you think it means to respect life? How do you show your respect?

I'll respect life.

June
11

"Laughter is the shortest distance between two people."

—Victor Borge

Do you have a good sense of humor? Can you make other people laugh? If not, maybe you need to grow a Funny Bone. Here are some tips from Earl Hipp:

- Watch funny movies.
- Read funny books.
- Listen to comedy albums.
- Laugh out loud into a recorder. Play it back when you feel blue.
- Learn a joke a week and share it with a friend.

TODAY

I'll laugh whenever and wherever I can.

June 12

"Kind words can be short and easy to speak, but their echos are truly endless."

—Mother Teresa

Do you remember the last time someone gave you a compliment? Perhaps they said you looked nice, or they recognized the hard work you had done. They might not have gone on and on about how great you are, but even a simple "thank you" can make you feel better about yourself. Can you make someone else feel good today, with a few short words?

TODAY

I'll give a compliment.

June
13

"There is no map for life; unfair things happen. The challenge is what you do with these things."

—Elizabeth Glaser

Being young doesn't protect you from life events that are sad and scary. What can you do about them? You can talk about them. Talk to your parents, teachers, or other adults you can trust. And learn what you can from these unfair life events. As Helen Keller said, "We could never learn to be brave and patient if there were only joy in the world."

TODAY

If I'm feeling sad or afraid, I'll talk with an adult I trust.

165

June 14

"It is better to be alone than in bad company."

—George Washington

Alan didn't even know that Eric was shoplifting. But when Eric got caught, Alan got in trouble, too. He had a hard time explaining to the police and his parents that he hadn't done anything wrong. Nobody believed him. He knew he had lost his parents' trust. When we choose friends who steal, do drugs, and act out in other ways, their reputation rubs off on us. Do you choose your friends wisely?

TODAY

**I'll think about
how I choose my friends.**

166

June
15

"When you do something you are proud of, praise yourself for it."

—Mildred Newman

Some people simply can't praise themselves. No matter how well they do something, they think it's not good enough. These people are perfectionists. If you have this problem, try this tip from perfectionism expert Miriam Adderholdt-Elliott: Go to a mirror and say, "I'm okay." It may feel weird at first, but keep doing it until you start believing it. Sooner or later, you will start believing it.

TODAY

I'll praise myself for something I'm proud of.

June 16

"Every man is the builder of a temple, called his body."

—Henry David Thoreau

If you were going to build a temple, what would you use? Potato chips and candy? French fries and ice cream? The foods you eat are your body's building-blocks. Especially now, when your body is growing, you need a well-balanced diet. You'll feel better. You'll look better. You'll think better. (Try fresh, natural foods to boost your brain power.)

TODAY

I'll make good choices about the foods I eat.

168

June
17

"Most of us ask for advice when we know the answer but want a different one."

—Ivern Ball

When Mom says you can't go out with your friends tonight, you ask Dad. When one friend tells you not to ignore the Keep Out sign at the construction site, you go with another friend who says it's okay. Deep down, you know the difference between right and wrong. But it's easy to find someone who will agree with you either way. Getting another person's approval doesn't make a wrong a right.

I won't ask for bad advice.

June
18

"I am the master of my fate;
I am the captain of my soul."

—W.E. Henley

Throughout your life, you will use your free will to say and do whatever you want. You may not always choose the right things, and you'll make mistakes along the way, but how else can you learn anything? You can't just sit back and say that fate will take care of you. That's too easy, and besides, it isn't true. Your life and your future are up to you.

TODAY

I'll make my own choices.

June 19

"Once upon a time in Spain there was a little bull and his name was Ferdinand... He liked to just sit quietly and smell the flowers."

—*The Story of Ferdinand*
(Munro Leaf)

If you're a bull, people expect you to look and act fierce. If you're a boy, people may expect you to be good at sports and bad at spelling. If you're a girl, people may expect you to be good at babysitting and bad at math. Other people's expectations can limit what you do. (Or you can surprise everybody and be yourself.)

TODAY

I'll meet my own expectations.

June 20

"I'm totally and absolutely fascinated by human nature. I like to go deep down inside myself to find out what's really there."

—Mary Stuart Masterson

Throughout the day, you're different things to different people. You're a son or daughter, a brother or sister, a friend or neighbor, a student or employee. How can you be all those things, yet still be yourself? Because your thoughts, feelings, dreams, and ideas are yours.

TODAY

**I'll forget about labels
and think about who I really am.**

172

June 21

"I don't know the key to success, but the key to failure is trying to please everybody."

—Bill Cosby

Y ou join scouts to please your parents. You play softball to please your friends. Do these scenarios sound familiar? So what are you doing to please yourself? What do you want to do? What means the most to you? Make room in your life for the things you choose just for you.

I'll please myself.

June 22

"Storms make trees take deeper root."

—Claude McDonald

You have the will to survive. You have the capability to withstand hardships and heartaches. You know that when someone betrays you, or a tragedy happens in your life, you feel lost and sad. But you also feel determined not to let the event destroy you. There is a powerful spirit inside you, a will to live and grow. That's what makes it possible for you to become stronger, even in emotional storms.

I'll recognize how strong I really am.

June
23

*"Nobody can be exactly like me.
Sometimes even I have trouble doing it."*

—Tallulah Bankhead

How much of you is the real you?
How much is a reflection of your friends? It's
hard to be true to yourself 100 percent of the
time. Especially when you're still growing
and changing. You may not even know who
the real you really is. What's important is to
be aware of influences like peer pressure.
Before you decide to fit in, check in with your
own feelings, values, and beliefs.

TODAY

**I'll think about ways in which I'm
different from my friends.**

June
24

"When you seek it, you cannot find it."

—Zen saying

Sometimes the things we want most in life are like fawns in a forest. The harder we look for them, the more we crash around, and the more they stay hidden. But if we sit very still, waiting quietly and patiently, the fawns may come to us. Leave yourself open for life's surprises. What you want may come to you.

TODAY

I'll let life surprise me.

June 25

"Life becomes a bore only if you lose your appetite for the future."

—Bette Davis

There are days when you don't know what to do with yourself. It's okay to be bored if you don't make a habit of it. When you're feeling low, go ahead and mope. Then, after an hour or two, get on with your life. Think of what's coming up in the next few weeks. Is there something you're really looking forward to? A vacation? A friend's visit? Free time? A party?

I'll look forward to something in my future.

June 26

"Do not commit the error...of assuming that if you cannot save the whole of mankind you have failed."

—Jan de Hartog

All around you are things that need fixing: pollution, homelessness, poverty, injustice. The list could go on and on. You may not be able to solve these problems single-handedly, but you can play a part. Don't put up with pollution. Pick up that empty bag and throw it away. Donate food or clothing to a local shelter. Accept people for who they are.

I'll begin to make a difference in the world.

June 27

"I never think about my limitations, and they never make me sad."

—Helen Keller

We all have limitations. There are things we can't do very well or at all. We also have choices when it comes to our limitations. We can think about them all the time and let them rule our lives. Or we can focus on our other abilities and talents. Helen Keller didn't let her limitations stop her. She went to college, wrote books, and was awarded the Presidential Medal of Freedom. (P.S. Today is Helen Keller's birthday.)

I'll focus on my talents.

June 28

"Be careful of your thoughts; they may become words at any moment."

—Iara Gassen

Words once spoken can't be taken back. Once you've said them, and another person has heard them, it's too late to change your mind. For the most part, this is all right. It's important to tell people how you're feeling and what you're thinking. But when it comes to lies, gossip, hurtful jokes, or criticism, be careful what you say. Think first and you won't have anything to regret later.

TODAY

I'll think before I talk about someone else.

June 29

"The greatest pleasure in life is doing what people say you cannot do."

—Walter Bagehot

"Don't try..." "You can't..." "Are you sure you want to..." "Here, let me do it for you..." "You're too young..." "What makes you think you can..." "That's not right for you..." "Forget it...." These are powerful words. They can wipe out your willpower. They can leave you feeling helpless and dependent. Don't let them. You know what you can do, no matter what anyone says.

TODAY

I'll trust my own abilities.

181

June 30

"There are only two ways to live your life. One is as though nothing is a miracle. The other is as though everything is a miracle."

—Albert Einstein

When you expect miracles, they happen. And when you live life as though everything is a miracle, this puts you in a wonderful frame of mind. Being alive is a miracle. Each sunrise is a miracle. Your cat's whiskers...your brother's goofy grin...your best friend's laugh...the breeze in the trees...a chocolate-chip cookie....

I'll expect a miracle.

July 1

"Be positive about yourself."

—Patti LaBelle

Virginia Satir has helped many people develop positive self-esteem. She says, "I want you to get excited about who you are, what you are, what you have, and what can still be for you. I want to inspire you to see that you can go far beyond where you are right now." Don't just accept yourself and your life. Get excited.

TODAY

I'll be positive about myself all day.

July 2

"Listen to the sounds of silence."

—Paul Simon

Sometimes you need to turn off the TV and the radio, close your books and close your eyes and just be still. Somewhere inside you is a calm, quiet place. You can leave your troubles outside. You can listen to the silence within yourself. You can find new strength and peace of mind. (If you don't know how to find that quiet place, turn to page 158 and try the meditation exercise.)

TODAY

**I'll visit the quiet place
inside myself.**

July 3

"Somebody's boring me...I think it's me."
—Dylan Thomas

Here it is, not even halfway through summer, and you're already bored out of your mind. You can blame it on your family and friends, but chances are you're really bored with yourself. And you're the only one who can change that. Read a book. Learn a skill. Make a friend. Find a hobby. Finish a project you started long ago. Comb your hair a different way. What else can you think of? (P.S. July is Anti-Boredom Month.)

TODAY

I'll do something to become more interesting to myself.

July 4

"I take a simple view of life: Keep your eyes open and get on with it."

—Laurence Olivier

Oscar Wilde once said, "Life is far too important a thing ever to talk about." Yet people talk about it endlessly. What is the meaning of life? What is our role in it? Where do we fit in? Are we important? And on and on. Sometimes we talk too much. It's a relief just to be quiet and take a simple view—to trust that we're here for a reason, and our lives have meaning.

I'll get on with my life.

186

July
5

"The more you know, the more you can create."

—Julia Child

For some people, talent seems to come naturally. They are "born" artists, athletes, writers, musicians, or math whizzes. They may be called "gifted." But look deeper and you'll find much more than a "gift." You'll find hard work, study, practice, and a strong desire to learn. These people have mastered the basics and gone beyond.

TODAY

I'll strengthen one of my talents by learning something new.

July 6

"Make a kid feel stupid and he'll act stupider."

—John Holt

"**Y**ou're dumb...." "You're so stupid...." "You never do anything right...." What can you do when someone puts you down? You can say, "I don't like to be talked to in that way." Then walk away. What if you can't say anything or walk away? Try positive self-talk. Tell yourself, "This person is wrong. My opinion of myself is the only one that matters." No one can make you feel stupid unless you let them.

TODAY

I won't let anyone make me feel stupid.

July 7

"It is never too late to give up our prejudices."

—Henry David Thoreau

We are all prejudiced. Some of us are more prejudiced than others. Some are prejudiced toward more people or groups. It's not easy to give up our prejudices—our biased, judging ways of seeing people. As long as we stay prejudiced, we don't have to take risks, ask questions, or learn anything new. (Taking risks, asking questions, and learning new things are all ways to start giving up prejudices, by the way.)

TODAY

I'll start giving up old prejudices.

189

July
8

"I celebrate myself, and sing myself."
—Walt Whitman

You've just been given an assignment: to celebrate yourself. You can do anything you want. Money is no object. So what will you do? Throw a party? Hire a band? Have your face printed on a thousand T-shirts? Put your picture on a billboard? Have someone write a song about you? Start a new town and name it after yourself? Make a movie of your life? Have a skywriter write your name in the clouds? Or...?

TODAY

I'll celebrate myself.

190

July 9

"Never go to bed mad. Stay up and fight."

—Phyllis Diller

Whenever James gets into an argument, he runs away. He stomps off to his room, slams the door, and won't come out. What's wrong with this scene? Problems don't get solved. People stay angry, and anger isn't healthy. Fighting doesn't just mean punching and shouting. It also means sticking up for yourself and standing up for what you believe in. Is there something in your life worth fighting for?

I won't keep my anger inside. I'll talk about it with someone I trust.

July 10

"Only a life lived for others is the life worthwhile."

—Albert Einstein

It's good to look out for yourself and your best interests. You need to know how to take care of yourself. But if that's all you think about, who will help those who need help? Find out today what you can do to make their lives more bearable. What's in it for you? A great feeling. So, in a way, you're doing it for yourself. (If not you, who? If not now, when?)

I'll help someone in need.

"The optimist sees the doughnut, but the pessimist sees the hole."

—McLandburgh Wilson

Are you an optimist or a pessimist? Do you see only the good or only the bad in life? Author Jonni Kincher says that the world needs both kinds of people—"optimists to give us encouragement, and pessimists to keep us cautious." If you're always optimistic, you may not be very practical. And if you're always pessimistic, you're probably not too happy. Can you find a balance between these two points of view?

I'll try to see things differently.

"You grow up the day you have your first real laugh—at yourself."

—Ethel Barrymore

Sam is skating with his friends when he trips over a crack in the sidewalk. Luckily, he lands in the grass. When his friends gather around, Sam looks up and says, "This seemed like a good place to rest. Want to join me?" He laughs, they laugh, and everyone feels okay. Sam knows how to laugh at himself. This wonderful skill can keep you from feeling angry, embarrassed, or ashamed. It can help other people feel comfortable around you.

TODAY

I'll try to laugh at myself.

July
13

"The difference between the impossible and the possible lies in a person's determination."

—Tommy Lasorda

Is there something you've always dreamed about doing? Something you've been planning for a long time? If you're determined, you can make anything happen. It might not happen tomorrow or even this year, but don't give up. Keep dreaming and planning. Your dreams can all come true.

I'll keep dreaming.

July 14

"Happiness is a conscious choice, not an automatic response."

—Mildred Barthel

You make many choices throughout each day. And, believe it or not, you choose your feelings. If you accept compliments without excuses, you've chosen to be happy. If you accept a difficult situation without complaining, you've chosen to be contented. For every new situation you face, you choose to be accepting or resentful. Which would you rather be?

TODAY

I'll choose to be happy.

July 15

"When you reach for the stars, you may not quite get one, but you won't come up with a handful of mud either."

—Leo Burnett

Will you choose to be mediocre? Or will you reach for the stars? Maybe you'll catch hold of one after all. You could be one of the world's great people—a leader who brings peace, a scientist who finds cures, an artist who creates beauty. Or maybe you'll fail; there's always that chance. How will you know unless you try?

TODAY

I'll believe in myself and say, "Yes, I can."

197

July 16

"Think for yourself. Whatever is happening at the moment, try to think for yourself."

—Jean Riboud

All your life, other people will tell you how to think. Parents, teachers, friends, bosses. Politicians and advertisers. Sometimes it's easier just to give in. Thinking for yourself can be hard work. You have to ask questions and find answers. You have to make decisions. Sometimes you have to defend what you think. Is it worth it? What do you think?

I'll make up my own mind about something. I won't just go along with the crowd.

July 17

"Well done is better than well said."
—Benjamin Franklin

"I've always wanted to...." "Someday I'm going to...." "If only I was older, I would...." How many times have you thought about starting something, only to find a reason to put it off? Why not start a project you've always talked about doing? Don't try to do it all at once, or in a single day. Start and finish one part at a time.

I'll do it, not just talk about it.

July 18

"If you want to kill time, why not try working it to death."

—O.A. Battista

There's nothing on TV...nowhere to go...no one to call....Are you bored? Then do something about it. It's amazing how fast time passes when you're busy. Ideas: Start that project early. Do a friend a favor. Volunteer at the park. Walk a neighbor's dog. List ten things you can do, then pick one and get it done. Being bored is a choice. If you don't like it, you can change it.

I'll choose to be busy instead of bored.

July
19

"There must be more to life than having everything!"

—Maurice Sendak

Imagine that you can have anything in the world you want—a fast car, a mansion, the latest video games, tons of money....It's fun to fantasize. Everybody does it. But problems arise when the "I-want-it" feeling takes control of your life. Instead, think of the things you already have. If there's something you don't need anymore, give it to someone who does. Cut down on your material wants, and you'll have energy (and money) to spare.

TODAY

I'll be contented with what I have.

July 20

"When you're through changing, you're through."

—Bruce Barton

One day Lucy was arguing with her mom. Lucy was getting angrier and angrier. Finally she yelled, "I'll never change!" Suddenly Lucy and her mom both started laughing. They knew that Lucy had just said a very silly thing. Everyone changes. We spend our whole lives changing. We learn new things. We meet new people. We have new ideas. An ancient Greek philosopher named Heraclitus once said, "There is nothing permanent except change."

TODAY

I'll welcome the changes in my life.

July 21

"The best thing parents can spend on their children is time, not money."

—Anonymous

Tracy's parents buy her anything she wants—clothes, games, jewelry. Tracy's friends think she's really lucky. But what if you knew that Tracy's parents hardly ever spend any time with her? Do your parents spend time with you? You have a right to some of their time and attention. If you're not getting enough, speak up. (Sometimes parents just need reminding.)

TODAY

I'll ask my mom or my dad to spend time with me. Maybe I'll think of something fun we can do together.

July 22

"To think is to differ."

—Clarence Darrow

Y ou've probably met all kinds
of people—people of different races,
backgrounds, and ages. Maybe you've
noticed that each person has his or her own
opinions. Maybe these don't always make
sense or seem right to you, but that's the way
the world works. A man named Walt McPhie
once said, "Whenever two people agree 100
percent, at least one of them isn't thinking."

TODAY

**I'll keep an open mind about
other people's ideas and opinions.**

"I don't think I could ever be close friends with anyone who didn't have a good sense of humor."

—Rob Reiner

Do your jokes fall flat? Do your attempts at humor make people mad or hurt their feelings? Humor teacher Jim Pelley recommends the A.T.T. Rule of Comedy: Humor must be Appropriate, Timely, and Tasteful. So when in doubt, ask yourself, "Am I laughing with people or at them?" Your humor goal should always be to improve, build up, and support, never to put down, tear down, or embarrass.

TODAY

I'll learn a new joke and share it with a friend.

"All sorrows can be borne if you tell a story about them."

—Karen Blixen

Is there something that makes you feel sad? A friendship gone wrong, a mistake left unfixed, a loss you can't cope with? You don't have to keep your sorrows locked inside yourself. Sometimes it helps to write about them. Often it helps to talk about them. Is there someone you can tell your story to? This may be a good day to find the friend who always listens, or the adult you can trust.

TODAY

I'll tell another person about something that's been bothering me.

"Be yourself. Who else is better qualified?"

—Frank J. Giblin, Jr.

It sounds easy, to "be yourself." In fact, it can be very hard. To be yourself, you have to know yourself. You have to stick up for yourself and resist peer pressure. You have to be willing to be lonely sometimes, and unpopular sometimes. Poet e.e. cummings once wrote, "To be nobody but yourself, in a world which is doing its best to make you like everybody else, means to fight one of the hardest battles of your life."

**I'll try to be myself,
as hard as it may be.**

July 26

"The Old Lady is left alone. Sadly she wonders: 'When shall I see my little Babar again?'"

—The Story of Babar the Little Elephant
(Jean de Brunhoff)

Have you ever had a friend who moved away? This can be a painful experience. But it doesn't have to mean the end of the friendship. You can write letters. You can send "cassette letters." (Record your favorite songs, tell jokes, and talk about your life, then send the cassette to your friend.) Save up for a long-distance phone call.

I'll get in touch with a friend
I feel lonesome for.

208

July 27

"Mistakes are a fact of life. It's the response to the error that counts."

—Nikki Giovanni

What do you do when you make a mistake? Blame yourself? Blame someone else? Try to hide it, ignore it, or forget it? These are all negative responses. Instead, try these positive responses: Admit your mistake to yourself and to another person you trust. If your mistake hurt someone else, do what you can to make up for it. Take responsibility for your mistake. This is the way to learn and grow.

TODAY

I'll respond positively to a mistake.

July 28

"Angels can fly because they take themselves lightly."

—G.K. Chesterton

Some people can't take a joke. They get angry when anyone teases them. They're always on the defensive, and their feelings are easily hurt. And they're not much fun to be around, because you always have to watch what you say. You want to tell them to lighten up, but you know they won't listen. (Is this something you need to work on for yourself?)

I'll lighten up.

July 29

"When a child loves you for a long, long time, not just to play with, but REALLY loves you, then you become Real."

—The Skin Horse in *The Velveteen Rabbit* (Margery Williams)

Love makes us real. It makes us feel alive and wanted and valued. It makes us feel good inside. Who are the people who love you? Write their names on a list. Fold it and put it in a special place. Take it out and look at it whenever you want to feel good inside.

I'll be thankful for the people who love me.

July 30

"As long as you can envision the fact that you can do something, you can do it— as long as you really believe it 100 percent."

—Arnold Schwarzenegger

Arnold Schwarzenegger is a world champion positive thinker. He started out as a body-builder and became Mr. Universe. He turned to acting and became a star. He is a successful business person and chairman of the President's Council on Physical Fitness and Sports. When he believes he can do something, he does it. (P.S. Today is Arnold Schwarzenegger's birthday.)

I'll believe in myself 100 percent.

July 31

"Muddy water, let stand, becomes clear."
—Lao Tzu

Imagine that you throw a coin into a stream. Then you take a stick and stir up the mud on the bottom. How can you find the coin? You can't until the water becomes clear again. You just have to wait. Some problems are like that: the harder you work to solve them, the messier they get. Sometimes you just need to be patient. When the "mud" settles, the solution may become clear.

TODAY

I'll practice being patient.

August 1

"I can't spend a single day now not making the most of things."

—Nigel Hawthorne

Are you making the most of each day of your life? This doesn't mean that you have to do something big, brave, or brand new every day. You don't have to reach an important decision or save the world. Sometimes making the most of a particular day means taking the day off.

**In my own way,
I'll make the most of the day.**

August 2

"We cannot become what we need to be by remaining what we are."

—Max De Pree

If things in your life are comfortable now, you may not want them to change. You may even resist change when it starts to happen. But think about this for a moment. Didn't change get you where you are today? Wasn't your life different last year and the year before? Today's changes may bring opportunities to make new friends, take new responsibilities, and win new freedoms.

I'll give change a chance.

August 3

"To feel valued, to know, even if only once in a while, that you can do a job well is an absolutely marvelous feeling."

—Barbara Walters

Think of the chores you do. Now think of one or more that you do especially well. Are you the world's best babysitter? Snow shoveler? Table setter? Are you a first-class fish tank cleaner? When we think of feeling proud, we usually picture ourselves doing something great. But you can also feel proud of the everyday, ordinary things you do.

TODAY

I'll do an everyday chore especially well.

August 4

"Let everyone sweep in front of his own door and the whole world will be clean."

—Johann von Goethe

Terese talks about saving the Earth. But she brings her school lunch in a plastic bag that she throws away. Carlo says he cares about the environment, but he leaves his radio turned on even when he's not at home. Real change takes a personal commitment from everyone. What simple steps can you take to live your own life more responsibly?

TODAY

I'll "precycle." I'll make sure something is recycled or recyclable before I use it or buy it.

August 5

"Why be influenced by a person when you already are one?"

—Martin Mull

And why be influenced by a crowd when you are an individual? It's hard to swim against the current of peer pressure. Sometimes it's almost impossible to be your own person and think your own thoughts. But if you want others to respect you for yourself, you must think and act for yourself. Try it for a day and see what it's like.

I'll think and act for myself.

August 6

*"I can live for two months on a
good compliment."*

—Mark Twain

Compliments should feel good. If they
make you feel uncomfortable—if you change
the subject, blush, or ignore compliments—
then you need practice accepting praise. The
next time someone gives you a compliment,
try this: Open your mouth and say "thanks."
Not "thanks, but..." or "it's nothing..." or "I
didn't do anything...." Just "thanks." It will
be over before you know it. It's easier than
you think.

TODAY

I'll accept a compliment.

August
7

"Sooner or later every one of us breathes an atom that has been breathed before by anyone you can think of who has lived before us—Michelangelo or George Washington or Moses."

—Jacob Bronowski

Sometimes when you're feeling out of it, lonely, and alone, it helps to remember that you're part of something much bigger than yourself. That something is life, a great, mysterious river with no beginning or end. Imagine breathing the atoms of heroes. Imagine your bones made up of the dust of the stars. Imagine the miracle you are.

TODAY

I'll enjoy just being alive.

August 8

"There are no shortcuts to any place worth going."

—Beverly Sills

"**I** wish I was older." "I wish I could do what other kids do." "I want to be an adult." Do you often hear yourself saying these words? Maybe you should slow down and enjoy your life the way it is. Think of all the things you can do today, right now. Take life a day at a time. You'll eventually get where you want to go.

I'll be happy with my life as it is right now.

August 9

"All things are possible until they are proved impossible—and even the impossible may only be so, as of now."

—Pearl S. Buck

Think of all the ordinary things that once seemed impossible—space flight, pocket calculators, 30-minute pizza deliveries. You used to think it would be impossible to read an entire book without pictures, and now see what you can do. Is there something in your life that seems impossible? Don't give up yet.

I'll remember that nothing is impossible.

August
10

"A hug is a perfect gift—one size fits all, and nobody minds if you exchange it."

—Ivern Ball

One day, Jon decided he was too grown-up for hugs. He was almost 12. When his friends saw him hugging his mom, they laughed. Jon was embarrassed. So he told his family to stop hugging him. They agreed, but they kept on hugging each other. Soon Jon started feeling left out and sad. He was grown-up enough to face his feelings. He decided that hugs were still okay. (Nobody is ever too grown-up for hugs.)

I'll give or get a hug.

August 11

"The less secure a man is, the more likely he is to have extreme prejudices."

—Clint Eastwood

Have you ever been discriminated against? Have you ever been kept from doing something you wanted to do, because you were the "wrong" race or sex or age? If you think you have been discriminated against, tell a trusted adult. (And remember your feelings so you don't discriminate against others.)

I'll learn more about discrimination.

August 12

"While forbidden fun is said to taste sweeter, it usually spoils faster."

—Abigail Van Buren ("Dear Abby")

When you learn that something is off limits, that makes it even more attractive. But use your common sense. Why would a parent or other adult forbid you to do a particular thing? Probably not because they want you to be unhappy. It's more likely that they care about you and want to keep you safe. If you wonder why something is off limits, ask.

TODAY

I'll obey the rules and trust that they were made to protect me.

August 13

"Be curious always! For knowledge will not acquire you; you must acquire it."

—Sudie Back

"Only the curious will learn," said Eugene S. Wilson. "And only the resolute will overcome the obstacles to learning." Not only do you have to want to learn. Sometimes you have to learn in spite of school—the noise, crowded classrooms, and overworked teachers. A new school year isn't too far away. What obstacles will you have to overcome this year? Who can help you?

I'll start thinking about the new school year. (What can I do to plan ahead?)

August 14

"Let your conscience be your guide."

—Jiminy Cricket

This is a true story: A young woman found a diamond bracelet in a department store bathroom. The bracelet was worth thousands of dollars. The young woman owed thousands of dollars in student loans. She thought about keeping the bracelet—who wouldn't? But she didn't keep it. The owner got her bracelet back. (Following your conscience may never make you rich, but it will always make you feel good about yourself.)

TODAY

I'll follow my conscience.

August
15

"One can never consent to creep when one feels an impulse to soar."

—Helen Keller

Dream big and follow your dreams. Don't let anyone hold you back. What seems impossible today might be possible tomorrow. Who knows? Whoever tells you that you can't do something doesn't know you. Encourage yourself and soar.

TODAY

I won't let anyone hold me back.

August 16

"One man's mess is another man's collection."

—*Shoe* (Jeff MacNelly)

Just think about the things people collect. Stamps, coins, cars, and cameras. Bugs, books, and baseball cards. Dolls, games, old clothes, furniture, autographs, postcards, rocks, shells, jokes, feathers, jars full of dirt....This list could go on forever. Do you have a collection? Do other people think it's dumb or weird? Who cares what they think? Keep collecting.

TODAY

I'll add to my favorite collection.

August
17

"I had the blues because I had no shoes, until upon the street I met a man who had no feet."

—Harold Abbott

Have you been feeling sorry for yourself lately? Maybe your parents don't understand you, or you don't have enough money to buy something you want, or you're sick of your sister, or your dog ate your favorite socks. And maybe it's time to put your problems in perspective. Rather than complain about how rotten your life is, get out and help someone who really has problems.

TODAY

I'll put my problems in perspective.

August 18

"There's no such thing as a free lunch."
—Milton Friedman

"**Y**ou can't get something for nothing." "If it sounds to good to be true, it probably is." You know these sayings, but do you believe them? When faced with a questionable ad or commercial, or a questionable friend, what do you do? Tip: Trust your gut feeling. If you feel uneasy or suspicious, there must be a reason. If you're unsure about something or someone, check it out before acting.

TODAY

I'll look before I leap.

231

August 19

"If you want peace, stop fighting."
—John-Roger and Peter McWilliams

There is always a war somewhere in the world. In times of war, kids feel powerless. (So do many adults.) It's true that you can't stop wars from happening. But you can make your own life more peaceful. Start at home. Instead of arguing, try talking and listening. Be more peaceful at school and in your neighborhood. And be more peaceful inside yourself. Try meditating, praying, or listening to quiet music. Come up with your own ideas.

TODAY

I'll be a more peaceful person.

August 20

"It only takes one person to change your life—you."

—Ruth Casey

If you don't like your life, what are you going to do about it? Even though you may be "just a kid," you still have choices. You can choose to feel good about yourself. You can choose to behave in ways that help you instead of hurt you. You are responsible for your feelings and behaviors. They belong to you.

I'll choose to feel good about myself.

233

August 21

*"I have a little shadow
that goes in and out with me,
And what can be the use of him
is more than I can see."*

—Robert Louis Stevenson

Do you have a "little shadow"—a younger kid who follows you around? This can be a pain. It's also a big responsibility. Your "shadow" may want to imitate you and be like you. Albert Schweitzer said, "Example is not the main thing in influencing others. It is the only thing."

TODAY

I'll set a good example.

August 22

"I knew what I wanted. That's why I haven't fallen apart."

—Patti D'Arbanville

Some people can't live without a firm plan or schedule. They need everything spelled out ahead of time, exactly the way it's going to be. Other people like to take things as they come—whatever happens, happens. Somewhere in the middle of these two extremes is a healthy state of mind. Learn to plan ahead, but leave room for surprises.

**I'll stay open to
new ideas and events.**

August 23

"God grant me the serenity to accept the things I cannot change, the courage to change the things I can, and the wisdom to know the difference."

—Reinhold Niebuhr

Millions of people say this prayer every day. Known as the Serenity Prayer, it's used in programs like Alcoholics Anonymous and Alateen, which help people who are recovering from addictions to alcohol or other drugs. But you don't have to be a program member to make this prayer part of your life. It's full of truth and hope for anyone at any age.

TODAY

I'll learn the Serenity Prayer.

August
24

"He who laughs, lasts."

—Mary Pettibone Poole

Laughter is good for your brain. It reduces stress and raises self-esteem. It boosts creativity and productivity. It builds empathy—the ability to experience other people's feelings as if they were your feelings. It helps to resolve conflict (how can two people stay mad if they're both laughing?). It gives you a new perspective on life. And those are just the mental benefits. To find out about the physical benefits, see page 147.

TODAY

**I'll make someone else laugh—
and join in.**

237

August
25

"I never dreamed of so much happiness when I was the ugly duckling."

—*The Ugly Duckling*
(Hans Christian Anderson)

The Ugly Duckling had an unhappy childhood. He didn't know that he would grow up to be a beautiful swan. You don't know your future, either. Some of your talents may still be hidden. Some of your interests are sure to change. And maybe you think you're an ugly duckling. Be patient. You will grow up. And you may find more happiness in the future than you ever dreamed.

TODAY

I'll look forward to my future.

August
26

"What a lovely surprise to finally discover how unlonely being alone can be."

—Ellen Burstyn

Who would have thought that being by yourself could be so much fun? When you're alone, you can decide what to do, what to think about, what to laugh at or cry about. Take a walk, write, read, stare into space, listen to music, laugh out loud—all of these things can be done alone.

I'll enjoy being alone.

August 27

"Good habits are as easy to form as bad ones."

—Tim McCarver

You know you should (pick one):
1. floss your teeth every day,
2. eat healthy snacks instead of junk food,
3. get more sleep,
4. read more,
5. turn in your homework on time,
6. exercise every day,
7. _____(fill in the blank).

What's wrong with starting today?

TODAY

I'll start a good habit.

August 28

"*Fear is the mind-killer. Unacknowledged fear is the worst kind of fear.*"

—Frank Herbert

There's plenty to fear in the world today. War and the threat of war. Violence and disease. If you sometimes (or often) feel afraid, no wonder. You can't do much to solve the world's problems. But you can do something to cope with your fears. Start by admitting them. Talk about them with people you trust. Learn as much as you can about the things you fear. These positive actions will help you to put your fears in perspective.

I'll name the things I fear.

August
29

"To carry a grudge is like being stung to death by one bee."

—William H. Walton

Rick is still mad at Barry for something that happened a year ago. Cassie can't forgive her mom for grounding her last month. Are you carrying a grudge? Why? You can't change the past. But you can keep a grudge from weighing you down another day. Forgive, forget, and get on with your life. Don't waste any more time and energy on something that just doesn't matter anymore.

TODAY

I'll let go of an old grudge.

August
30

"Recall it as often as you wish, a happy memory never wears out."

—Libbie Fudim

It won't be long before school starts again (if it hasn't already). When you think back on the summer, what is your happiest memory? When was the best time? What was your favorite thing to do? The greatest place to be? If this is a memory you share with a friend, you may want to write it down. Then make a copy for your friend.

TODAY

I'll think of a happy memory from the summer.

August
31

"To make your ideas work for you, you first have to work for them."

—Thomas Alva Edison

Thomas Edison had a head full of ideas. He was also a hard worker. It was Edison who said the famous words, "Genius is one percent inspiration and ninety-nine percent perspiration." He left behind more than 3,000 notebooks and 1,000 patents for his inventions. If Edison had been a lazy man, we might not have electric lights, phonographs, or movies.

TODAY

I'll work for one of my ideas.

September 1

"People change and forget to tell each other."

—Lillian Hellman

One day your best friend likes the same things you do. The next day you can't agree on anything. What happened? Change. "As children become teenagers, their interests change," educators Larry and Cindy Putbrese explain. "When interests change, friendships change....Many young people don't understand this yet. They feel badly because they get left out or believe they have done something wrong. It helps to understand that changing friends is a normal, if sometimes painful, part of growing up."

TODAY

I'll accept a change in a friend.

245

September
2

"A challenge is something you haven't done before that you work towards."

—Sarah Jessica Parker

You're facing a new situation and it scares you. Maybe you're in a new school this year and you're feeling lost. Maybe you're not sure about your new teacher. Maybe there's been a big change in your family. Whatever the situation, you know you can handle it. Whatever the challenge, you can cope.

I'll face a new situation head on.

September
3

"People are as free as they want to be."

—James Baldwin

How free do you want to be? Has a bad habit or unhealthy relationship taken away your freedom? You can get it back. If you need help breaking a habit or ending a relationship, talk to a trusted adult. But mostly, believe in yourself. You know you can make it on your own. Oprah Winfrey says, "The only thing that can free you is the belief that you can be free."

TODAY

If I have let a habit or
relationship run my life,
I'll start taking back my freedom.

September
4

"Ninety percent of the way you feel is determined by how you want to feel."

—John Kozak

You can store good feelings in a self-esteem "savings account." Gershen Kaufman and Lev Raphael tell how:

1. Write down five things you did today which you feel proud of. (These don't have to be big, important things. You might write, "I took out the garbage without being told.")
2. Do this every day.
3. Keep your I-Did-It Lists in a special place.
4. Whenever you want to feel good, read through your I-Did-It Lists.

I'll start an I-Did-It List.

September
5

"He who praises everybody praises nobody."

—Samuel Johnson

Some people try too hard to be friendly. They go along with their friends on everything, no questions asked. They lose their individuality as they work to please their friends. In the end, their friends don't respect them, and they don't respect themselves. In real friendships, there are boundaries. Real friends don't always agree. And they don't take advantage of each other or use each other.

TODAY

I'll be a real friend.

September
6

"No matter how big or soft or warm your bed is, you still have to get out of it."

—Grace Slick

This morning, when you woke up, did you wish you could stay in bed with the covers over your head? You'll feel more like jumping out of bed tomorrow if:

1. you get enough sleep tonight,
2. you're ready to face the day (homework done, school stuff ready), and
3. you feel good about yourself.

TODAY

I'll make sure I'm ready for tomorrow.

September
7

"There are no second acts in American lives."

—F. Scott Fitzgerald

Some people do their best at whatever they do. Others slide through life, barely making it and not seeming to care. Which kind are you? Are you making the most of your abilities? Or are you wasting your time and your talents? You can make a change. Start small. Do the extra-credit homework. Finish your chores without complaining (and do them right). Surprise someone by doing a favor. Turn your life around.

TODAY

I'll start being my best.

September
8

"I like the idea of us all being here."

—Gwendolyn Brooks

A science fiction writer wrote a story about the Earth of the future. There was only one race, and everyone's skin was gray. How boring the world would be if we were all alike! Luckily there are many different races, peoples, ethnic groups, countries, cultures, colors, foods, faiths, types of music, dances, clothing, languages, houses, paintings, poems, churches, eyes, noses, hair styles....What is your ethnic background? What do you like best about your roots?

TODAY

**I'll feel proud of myself
and my people.**

September
9

"They can transport my BODY to school, but they can't chain my SPIRIT! My spirit roams free! Walls can't confine it! Laws can't restrain it! Authority has no power over it!"

—Calvin in *Calvin and Hobbes*
(Bill Watterson)

Sometimes school isn't very interesting. You'd rather be anywhere else. But you're stuck there...or are you? Teacher Wes Beach says, "Your inner world is a place you can go whenever you want to." Find time to daydream. Use a free period to doodle, write a poem, or stare into space. Get away for a while, and you'll come back refreshed.

TODAY

I'll visit my inner world.

253

September
10

"Don't quit five minutes before the miracle happens."

—Anonymous

Runners call it "hitting the wall." They've been running and running, and suddenly it feels like they just can't take another step. But they do. You may feel like you just can't write that paper over again, or practice your trumpet one more time, or shoot one more basket, or struggle for one more minute with a math problem you don't understand. But you can.

TODAY

I won't be a quitter.

September
11

"In times like these, it helps to remember that there have always been times like these."

—Paul Harvey

With support and love from others, you can usually face anything that comes your way. But when you turn away from others and withdraw into yourself, a bad situation can get worse. You may think you have no one to turn to, but think again. Look around; the same people who helped you before are waiting to help you again.

TODAY

I'll ask for help if I need it.

255

September 12

"When things go wrong, don't go with them."

—Anonymous

Going along with the crowd can give you a sense of belonging. It can also get you into trouble. You've heard about kids who were caught up in crimes because they got mixed up with the wrong people. But what about the crowd who decides to tease the new kid in school? Or throws a party when parents are away? Are you wise enough to know when things are going wrong, and strong enough to stand your ground?

TODAY

I won't go along with something that doesn't feel right to me.

September
13

"I make the most of all that comes and the least of all that goes."

—Sara Teasdale

Welcome new opportunities. Leave past mistakes behind. As Satchel Paige said, "Don't look back. Somethin' might be gaining on you." Look to the future with excitement and hope. Start the new school year with this attitude, and you're sure to have the best year of your life.

I'll make the most of
everything that comes my way.

257

September
14

"When I think of the hundreds of things I might be, I get down on my knees and thank God that I'm me."

—Elsie Janis

You are unique. There's no one else like you, anywhere in the world. No one else has exactly your abilities. No one else has exactly your talents. No one else has your potential. Think of the hundreds of things you might be, and the hundreds of things you already are.

TODAY

I'll feel thankful for my abilities, talents, and potential.

September
15

"Sometimes, if you're hurrying so much to see what's for tomorrow, you miss what's for today."

—Demi Moore

Y ou just started a new school year, but you can't wait until next year, when you're older. Or maybe it's Monday morning, but all you can think about are your plans for the coming weekend. Do you spend a lot of your time waiting for things to happen? Meanwhile, what's happening to your time?

TODAY

I'll pay attention to today.

September 16

"One cannot be first in everything."

—Aesop

Cassie never lost a spelling bee—until sixth grade, when she blew it in the final round. The winner was a boy named Daryl. Cassie didn't know it, but Daryl liked her. So when Cassie burst into tears and ran out of the room, Daryl felt terrible, too. Cassie thought she had to be the best at everything, and that made her a sore loser. Humorist Will Rogers once said, "We can't all be heroes because somebody has to sit on the curb and clap as they go by."

TODAY

I'll praise another person's success.

September
17

"The ability to concentrate and to use your time well is everything."

—Lee Iacocca

The TV is on, the phone is ringing, your brother's boombox is blaring heavy metal, your cat is biting your toes—no wonder you can't concentrate on your homework. Is there a quiet, private place you can turn into your home study center? You'll need good lighting, a desk or table, a straight-backed chair, and a "Do Not Disturb" sign.

TODAY

I'll think about where I do my homework. Are there too many distractions? Can I find a better place to work?

September
18

"It takes a friend and an enemy to really hurt you: the enemy to say something rotten about you, and the 'friend' to tell you about it."

—Abigail Van Buren ("Dear Abby")

People spread stories about each other for many reasons. Jealousy, peer pressure, and meanness are just a few. The most hurtful stories are those that come from so-called "friends." You may think you're helping someone when you repeat an ugly story you've heard. You may think you're just being honest. A Roman poet named Lucan once said, "Honesty is often in the wrong."

TODOY

I'll let an ugly story or rumor end with me.

262

September 19

"My teachers liked me a lot, but I could never really trust them. I was afraid that one day they would see the real me—the unlikeable person I thought I was."

—Steven, 12

Do you feel like a fake? Do you worry that others will find out about the real you? If you have these feelings, you're not alone. In fact, these feelings are so common that they have a special name: The Impostor Syndrome. If you think you're an "impostor," tell an adult you trust. Get help dealing with these feelings.

TODAY

I'll list five great things about the real me.

September
20

"You can't hit a home run unless you step up to the plate. You can't catch fish unless you put your line in the water. You can't reach your goals if you don't try."

—Kathy Seligman

Fill in the blanks: "I can't (1)_____ unless I (2)_____." Now switch (1) and (2) around to finish this sentence: "When I (2)_____ I will (1)_____." Which feels better to you? Which makes your goal seem more reachable? What happens when you try this with other personal goals?

TODAY

I'll think positively about a personal goal.

264

September
21

"Things could be a lot worse."

—Joyce Carol Oates

What's your greatest gripe? School? Friends who bug you? Adults who don't understand you? No money? No freedom? The wrong clothes? Your problems and concerns are real to you. But are you spending all of your time complaining? If you're not sick, if you're not homeless, if you're not cold or hurt or lonely, then things really could be a lot worse for you.

I'll be thankful for my life.

September
22

"I think I can—I think I can—I think I can—I think I can—"

—*The Little Engine That Could*
(Watty Piper)

It may seem silly, but telling yourself "I think I can..." really works. It puts you in the mood to succeed. It raises your self-esteem. This is an example of positive self-talk. You can use positive self-talk to help solve problems. You're more likely to make good decisions when you're feeling good about yourself.

I'll practice positive self-talk.

September
23

"Observe things as they are and don't pay attention to other people."

—Huang Po

What happens when you see things one way, and your friends see them another way? It's hard to trust your own perceptions when people you care about disagree with you. It's hard to hold on to your own beliefs when others insist that you're crazy or wrong. It's easier to give in—and give up part of yourself. A wise woman named Louise Hay once said, "Part of self-acceptance is releasing other people's opinions."

I'll trust my own perceptions.

September
24

"The trouble with the rat race is that even if you win, you're still a rat."

—Lily Tomlin

You've probably heard adults talk about the "rat race"—the struggle to get ahead by competing with others. Adults aren't the only ones who compete. Think about school tests, sports teams, popularity contests, grades, and playground games, for starters. One way to escape from the junior rat race is by learning to cooperate. Do you know any cooperative games? If you don't, ask your teacher or look in the library.

TODAY

**I'll try cooperating
instead of competing.**

September
25

"You must learn to say no when something is not right for you."

—Leontyne Price

Do you know how to say no? This one little word can keep you out of trouble. It can keep you from getting stressed out or burned out. It can make you feel good about yourself. You can practice saying no in front of a mirror. Stand up straight. Put a serious look on your face. Put an I-mean-it tone in your voice. Put your hands on your hips, if that helps. Then say it again and again: "No." "No." "NO!"

TODAY

I'll practice saying no.

September
26

"Friendship is the only cement that will ever hold the world together."

—Woodrow Wilson

Each new school year is a chance to make new friends. This year, look beyond the ordinary places. Most of your friends will probably be at school, but they don't all have to be. Most will probably be around your age, but this isn't a requirement. What about your brother or sister, an elderly relative, or the next door neighbor? All are potential friends.

TODAY

I'll stop and talk to someone I'd normally pass by.

270

September 27

*"Everybody, sooner or later, sits down
to a banquet of consequences."*

—Robert Louis Stevenson

When we hear the word
"consequences," we usually think of
something unpleasant. (As in, "You did it!
Now you'll have to suffer the consequences.")
But consequences don't have to be bad. The
original meaning of the word was "something
that follows closely." Bad doesn't follow
good. If your actions are positive and right,
the consequences will be, too.

I'll think ahead about the
consequences of my actions.

September
28

"Creation is everything you do. Make something."

—Ntozake Shange

Make a painting or a mud pie. Make a wish or a decision. Make a model, a mess, or a mistake. Make up your mind, a song, or a story. Just make something today. Put your whole self into it. Get lost in it. See what happens. People talk about "creative power" and "creative energy." Do you have it? Can you feel it?

TODAY

I'll make something.

September
29

"It does not matter how slowly you go so long as you do not stop."

—Confucius

It's frustrating when things don't go the way you want them to, or happen as fast as you wish. Like that school project. A new friendship. Or maybe you're working on rebuilding trust that was lost when you didn't keep a promise. Another Chinese philosopher, Lao Tzu, once said, "The journey of a thousand miles begins with one step."

TODAY

I'll take a step toward a goal that matters to me.

September
30

"The harder you work, the luckier you get."

—Gary Player

Would you like to be a lucky duck? Then get in the water and swim. Nobody becomes successful due to luck alone. Nobody aces a quiz, wins a swim meet, or gets elected class president because they're lucky. Oprah Winfrey (herself a great success story) says, "Luck is a matter of preparation meeting opportunity." You'll have many chances to shine. Be ready, and you'll be "lucky," too.

TODAY

I'll make my own good luck.

October 1

"Grant that I might not criticize my neighbor until I have walked a mile in his moccasins."

—Louise Garfield Monroe

Trevor falls asleep in class. Katie wears weird clothes. Eric is a teacher's pet. Trisha is a troublemaker. Do you know kids like these? They're easy to criticize. But people aren't the way they are for no reason. We are all shaped by the circumstances of our lives. How much do you really know about the outsiders in your school? If you knew more about them, would your opinions change?

I'll try to be more understanding of others.

October 2

"If at first you doubt, doubt again."

—William Bennett

You're not sure about the party your friends told you about, but you promise to think about going. You know you can find out the answers to a quiz, but you're worried about getting caught. You think your parents would believe your lie, yet you hesitate to tell it. What should you do? When you're faced with choices like these, go with your gut feeling. And if your gut feeling says "no," don't talk yourself into saying "yes."

TODAY

**I'll trust my feelings
and do what I feel is right.**

276

October 3

"You know, when you're young and curious, people love to teach you."

—Dede Allen

You may think that school is a bore. Some days (maybe most), it is. But try looking at it from another angle. This is the only time in your life when learning will be your main responsibility. (It may seem hard, but it's easier than paying rent or buying groceries.) Show some interest, show some respect, do your school work, don't act up, and most teachers will go out of their way to help you.

TODAY

I'll go to school with a good attitude.

October 4

"An old pond—
The sound of the water
When a frog jumps in."

—Basho

Can you hear that sound? Use your imagination to picture a frog, sitting on the side of a pond...suddenly he jumps! Is the sound a "splash," or more of a "ker-plunk"? Can you see the ripples spread across the water? Are there lily pads floating on the pond? Do little fish swim below the surface of the water? Is the sun shining? Aren't you glad you have an imagination?

TODAY

I'll enjoy my imagination.

October 5

"I auditioned for everything. I was never picked immediately, but I always tried."

—Diane Keaton

There's no such thing as an overnight success. Ask any successful person. Most rock stars spend years in no-name bands. Actors take bit parts in community theaters. Athletes start on neighborhood teams. If you want to succeed, you'll have to work hard, too. Maybe you already do. Keep trying and don't give up.

TODAY

**I'll work hard
for something I want.**

October 6

"Our prime purpose in this life is to help others. And if you can't help them at least don't hurt them."

—The Dalai Lama

To some people, hurting and being hurt is a way of life. They have learned it from adults, who learned it when they were growing up. It isn't easy to break out of this cycle of pain. It takes time, hard work, and a lot of help. If you feel that people are hurting you, physically or emotionally, tell an adult you trust. Get help.

TODAY

I'll remember that words can hurt.

October 7

"If you don't stand for something, you will stand for anything."

—Ginger Rogers

Do you ask other people for their opinions before you form your own? Do you go along with whatever they say? It's good to keep an open mind, and even to change your mind, if that's what you want. It's not good to be wishy-washy or easily influenced by others. Decide what you stand for, then stand behind your decision. People will respect you for it.

TODAY

I'll decide for myself what I stand for.

October 8

"Be brave enough to accept the help of others."

—Melba Cosgrove

Many young people have trouble in school because they don't or won't ask for help. They worry about their friends making fun of them. They're embarrassed to admit that they don't understand an assignment or can't figure out a problem. Their troubles pile up until it seems too late to do anything about them. It's never too late. But it's a lot easier if you get help as soon as you need it. Don't wait.

TODAY

If I need help with my school work, I'll ask for it.

October 9

"If you allow the law of 'an eye for an eye,' very soon the only people around are going to be blind."

—Desmond M. Tutu

When a friend says something mean to you or betrays your trust, what's your first reaction? You might feel like getting even. But will that really solve anything? Or will it make things worse? Revenge never heals hurts. Instead of striking back, go off and cool down. Later, tell your friend how you feel about what happened. If you want an apology, ask for one. If your friend wants forgiveness, give it.

TODAY

I'll resist the urge to get even.

October 10

*"You're right from your side,
I'm right from mine."*

—Bob Dylan

When you disagree with someone, are you able to see both sides? This is a wonderful skill to have. Few things in life are all right or all wrong. When you can understand another person's point of view, you are closer to reaching an agreement. You can compromise, maybe even work together. (Maybe your sides aren't so different after all.) One way to learn this skill is by joining a debate team. Does your school have a debate team?

TODAY

**I'll try to see an issue or problem
from both sides.**

284

October 11

"No one can make you feel inferior without your consent."

—Eleanor Roosevelt

What happens when other people make fun of you or put you down? Do you accept what they say and let it ruin your day? Now ask yourself this question: What makes them the experts on you? You don't have to listen to them. And you certainly don't have to agree with them. Your opinion of yourself is the only one that counts. (P.S. Today is Eleanor Roosevelt's birthday.)

TODAY

I'll refuse to feel inferior.

October 12

"We all live under the same sky, but we don't have the same horizon."

—Konrad Adenauer

How can we prevent wars? How should we feed the hungry? What's the best way to get rid of garbage? Everyone has different ideas for solving these world problems. We all live on the same planet, but we don't always agree on how to live on it. Listen to as many views as you can. Learn as much as you can. Then form your own opinions and ideas.

TODAY

I'll write down my ways for solving world problems.

"Humor has the power to turn any situation around.

—Allen Klein

Humor can help put your problems in perspective. Problems don't seem as big or scary when you're laughing and relaxed. Try these humorous ways to approach a problem that's been bothering you:

1. Ask yourself how your favorite cartoon character would solve your problem.
2. Smile for a count of ten; stop smiling for a count of ten; repeat. You'll feel more relaxed and ready to face your problem.
3. If you get stuck, take a bubble-blowing break.

**I'll use humor
to help solve a problem.**

October 14

*"I don't just want to be successful.
I want to have fun."*

—Julie Brown

Everyone has an idea of what success
means to them. Some people think it's having
a lot of money, a good job, and a family.
Others define success as peace of mind. Most
people agree that success takes hard work.
As you work for your own definition of
success, remember to stop and have fun along
the way. (All work and no play makes you
dull, dull, dull.)

I'll have fun.

288

October 15

"Wherever you are, it is your friends who make your world."

—William James

Is your world of friends limited to your school, your neighborhood, or your town? There's a fun and easy way to make friends around the world: Pen pals. Start by writing to the Information Center on Children's Cultures, The U.S. Committee for UNICEF, 331 E. 38th St., New York, NY 10016. If you send them a self-addressed, stamped envelope, they'll send you an international list of pen pal agencies.

TODAY

I'll think of a country where I'd like to have a friend.

"Confidence is what makes me different from guys at home."

—Will Smith

Have you ever noticed how much influence you have over yourself? If you tell yourself that you're too weak, ugly, or dumb to accomplish something, then that's the way you'll feel, and you'll probably fail. But if you tell yourself that you can do it, you're likely to succeed. Positive self-talk can help you believe in yourself.

TODAY

I'll use only positive self-talk— no negative thoughts or words.

October 17

"I live a life that pleases me."

—Olivia de Havilland

Everyone wants to be liked. It's easy to go along with the crowd and blend in with others. As long as you're in a group, you feel safe and comforted. But is being with the group, and doing what the group does, always the best way? What if you feel like staying home one night when your friends want to go out? Although it might be easier to go, who says you can't say no? Be your own person. Please yourself.

TODAY

I'll be an individual.

October 18

"Be gentle with all who are weak and helpless in this world."

—Jesus

There's a tradition in most schools, and maybe in yours: The big kids pick on the little kids. You've been a little kid, and you've been picked on. Now you're becoming a big kid. What will you do?

TODAY

I'll remember that I used to be little. I'll remember what it felt like to be picked on.

October 19

"Honesty is the best policy and spinach is the best vegetable."

—Popeye

You've seen what happens when Popeye eats a can of spinach. His muscles pop out of his arms. His fists move so fast they blur. He's strong enough to save Olive Oyl and clobber Bluto. Honesty gives you "moral muscles." When you're honest, you're always on the right side of an argument. Your friends and parents trust you. (And you don't even have to eat spinach.)

TODAY

I'll be honest.

October 20

"Yakety-yak.
Don't talk back!"

—Jerry Leiber and Mike Stoller

"Children should be seen and not heard." Let's throw out that saying, and good riddance to bad rubbish. Your feelings count. Your opinions matter. And your words deserve to be heard. You have a right to question authority, if you think the authorities are wrong. You have a right to stick up for yourself with your parents and your teachers. What's the key to being heard? Be polite and respectful. Be willing to listen, too.

TODAY

I'll speak out about something that's bothering me.

October 21

"I'm finding that what my job on earth really involves is spreading a little sunshine around. You can't help but get the sunshine back."

—George Hamilton

Have you noticed that when you smile, others near you start smiling, too? And when you're depressed and frowning, others seem to catch your blue mood? Nobody expects you to be happy all the time. But a bright, cheerful outlook will make life much more pleasant for you and everyone around you.

TODAY

I'll choose to be cheerful.

O*ctober* 22

"In the face of an obstacle which is impossible to overcome, stubborness is stupid."

—Simone de Beauvoir

"**I**f at first you don't succeed, try, try again." Most of us learn this saying when we are very young. We learn that it's shameful to give up and give in. But sometimes it's smart to know when to quit. Quitting doesn't always equal defeat. It can be a positive, healthy choice.

TODAY

If I have been trying to do the impossible, I'll decide to keep trying—or quit.

October 23

"Somewhere, something incredible is waiting to be known."

—Carl Sagan

The future can be frightening. But knowledge can help you manage your fears. Although you can't know what the future will bring, you can make it less frightening by planning for it. It's not too soon to start thinking about jobs and careers. Will you want to go to college? Many young people start finding out about colleges in middle school. Who can help you with your future plans? Your parents? School counselors? Anyone else?

TODAY

I'll start planning for my future.

October
24

"Sometimes I sits and thinks, and sometimes I just sits."

—Anonymous

School, chores, work, family, friends, hobbies, homework, sports, lessons....Are you so busy that you never have a minute for yourself? Does it seem like every second of your life is planned out and filled in? Everyone needs "sits and thinks" time for relaxing, solving problems, and daydreaming. How can you get some?

TODAY

**I'll take 15 minutes
to just sit and think.**

October 25

"Nobody had faith in me. They said I would fail...but it made me rebellious."

—Kelly McGillis

Many people in your life are more than willing to encourage you. They are ready to help you in any way they can. But some won't be able to see your abilities and potential. They will try to discourage you from following your dreams. Jacob Neusner says, "Do not let people put you down. Believe in yourself and stand for yourself and trust yourself."

TODAY

**I won't let anyone put me down.
I'll believe in myself.**

299

October
26

"There's only one corner of the
universe you can be certain of improving
and that's your own self."

—Aldous Huxley

Most of us are good at telling other
people what's wrong with them. We know
how they could be better parents, friends,
brothers or sisters, if only they would listen to
us. In fact, you can't change other people.
Their behaviors, thoughts, and feelings are
theirs, like yours are yours. But you can
change yourself, if there's something you
want to change. Tip: Start small, and don't
expect perfection.

TODAY

I'll make a small but positive
change in myself.

300

October 27

"The first problem for all of us, men and women, is not to learn, but to unlearn."

—Gloria Steinem

Are all smart people 90-pound weaklings? Are all rich people snobs? Are all politicians dishonest? Of course not. You know better. But you probably recognize these stereotypes. Have you ever been hurt by a stereotype? Have people made judgments about you because of your age, race, religion, sex, family, or some other factor, without even knowing the real you? Are there any stereotypes you need to unlearn?

TODAY

I'll refuse to think in stereotypes.

October
28

"Growing pains are real."

—Morris Sklansky

Your body is changing. Your emotions are changing. Your relationships are changing. Your whole life is changing. Some adults may tell you, "Oh, you're just having growing pains." They may act as if your "growing pains" aren't very important. But they are important. Some adults will respect your growing pains. They will listen to you talk about them. They will help you to understand them. Do you know any adults like these?

TODAY

**I'll make a list of three adults
I feel comfortable talking to.**

October 29

"Always do what you say you are going to do. It is the glue and fiber that binds successful relationships."

—Jeffrey A. Timmons

Your friends have always been there for you. Friends are such a big part of your life that you may begin to take them for granted. You might forget that they deserve respect and that they trust you to tell them the truth. Be thankful for your friends. They've helped you in the past; treat them with respect and they'll be there for you in the future.

TODAY

**I'll thank a friend
for being my friend.**

October
30

"For fast-acting relief, try slowing down."
—Lily Tomlin

Many young people try to do too
much, too soon. They try to grow up too fast.
For some, this means using alcohol and other
drugs. For others, it means having sex before
they're ready. It's okay to slow down. It's
okay to stop. And it's okay to ask for help
with problems you can't handle yourself.

TODAY

I'll take things slowly.

304

October
31

"Don't love anything that can't love you back."

—Noreen Briggs

Finish this sentence: "I love...." Do you think of things or people? Places or people? Sports or people? Hobbies or people? Only people can love you back. "Love" is a word we often waste. We talk about "loving" movies or clothes, videos or chocolate. Who are the people you love who love you back? How do you show your love for one another?

**I'll be extra loving
toward the people I love.**

November
1

"The heart has reasons that the mind has no knowledge of."

—Pascalli

When you make a decision, do you follow your head or your heart? Your brains or your feelings? Logic or emotions? Maybe that depends on the kind of decision it is. What's important is to know that you can use both. Some people think that decisions based on feelings aren't any good. They will encourage you to use your head and ignore your feelings. They might say, "Don't be so emotional." But your emotions matter.

I'll listen to my head and my heart.

November
2

"The time is always right to do what is right."

—Dr. Martin Luther King, Jr.

Twyla hated it when her friends teased Deborah. It wasn't Deborah's fault that she was big and clumsy and slow. Usually she didn't even know she was being teased. If the other girls laughed, Deborah laughed, too. She didn't realize they were laughing at her. This made Twyla crazy. She was going to tell her friends to quit teasing Deborah. She was just waiting for the right time.

TODAY

If I see a wrong being done, I'll do what is right.

November
3

"The applause is secondary; when you feel like you're delivering, that's the most exciting part."

—Shauna Rolston

Why do people get up on stage or stand in front of a camera and perform? For many, the love of acting or music or making people laugh is what keeps them going. The reviews aren't as important as being able to do something they enjoy. Sometime during your busy schedule, make time to do something you enjoy. Don't do it for praise or recognition. Do it because you enjoy it.

I'll do something just for me.

November
4

"Change comes slowly."

—Paul McCartney

Some days, it seems like everything about your life is wrong. You wish you could change it all, starting with yourself. Maybe you want to lose ten pounds or gain ten pounds, build a stronger body or a sharper mind. Maybe you want to get along better with your family or make new friends. These kinds of changes take time. Be patient with yourself. You'll get there.

I'll accept that
change comes slowly.

November
5

"Goals determine what you're going to be."

—Julius Erving

How does someone get to be a successful actor, singer, athlete, politician, or writer? Those men and women you read about and see on TV worked hard for their fame and endured many years of failure. But they all kept their goals in mind as they were rejected, criticized, or ignored. How about you? Are you willing to struggle to achieve your goals?

TODAY

I'll focus on my goals.

November
6

"There is more to life than increasing its speed."

—Mohandas Gandhi

Are you feeling stressed and over-scheduled? Jim Delisle and Judy Galbraith recommend this step-by-step solution:

1. List all the activities you're involved in (and have some control over).
2. Rank them according to how important they are to you.
3. Put your list away for a week to 10 days.
4. Create a new list with new rankings.
5. Compare your two lists.
6. Decide which activities you can cut out of your life.

TODAY

**I'll do something to
slow down my life.**

November
7

"God gave burdens, also shoulders."

—Yiddish proverb

We all have problems. We all have responsibilities. We're all on schedules. And sometimes, we all feel loaded down, as if our lives are too busy, our problems too heavy, our responsibilities too big. Is there someone whose shoulder you can lean on, even cry on? Are you a good shoulder for your friends? Hubert Humphrey once said, "The greatest healing therapy is friendship and love."

TODAY

I'll be a good friend.

312

November
8

"Feelings aren't 'wrong' or 'right,' 'bad' or 'good.' Feelings just are."

—Gershen Kaufman and Lev Raphael

People like to label their feelings. Happiness is "good." Jealousy is "bad." Anger is "wrong"—unless it's for a good reason, which makes it "right." Labels get in the way of what we're really supposed to do with our feelings: feel them, accept them, and be responsible for them.

I won't label my feelings.

November 9

"You must first please yourself...and thereafter, only people you care about. Those who try to please everyone end up pleasing no one."

—Sol Gordon

Paul is a people-pleaser. He is always doing favors for his friends. He runs errands for his teachers. He volunteers for everything. And he often feels anxious and afraid. In trying to please everyone, Paul is hurting himself. He needs to stop and figure out what he wants and needs.

I'll remember that I can't please everyone, and I don't have to try.

November 10

"You don't have to be grown-up to do something worthwhile."

—Jennifer Engel

Some people may think you're "just a kid," but you can still make a difference in the world. Teacher Barbara Lewis says, "You have a fresh view of life. You don't know all the reasons why something won't work. You're willing to try new things. You come up with new ideas. And you have your own opinions." What would you like to work on?

TODAY

I'll think of ways to make a difference in the world. Maybe I'll choose one to work on.

November 11

*"Nature has created us with the
capacity to know God, to experience God."*

—Alice Walker

What do you think about when you think about God? Going to church or temple? Saying grace before meals or prayers before bedtime? Quiet thought and meditation? Most people believe in a higher power; many call that higher power God. They feel the need to find more meaning in life than they can see on the surface. They want to know that they're not alone in the universe. What are you doing to take care of your spiritual self?

TODAY

**I'll spend time with
my spiritual self.**

November 12

"Today's opportunities erase yesterday's failures."

—Gene Brown

Every day is a fresh new start filled with new opportunities. No matter what you said or did yesterday, last week, or last year, today you can start fresh. If you did something you're sorry about, start today by forgiving yourself. If you said something to hurt another person, start today by apologizing. If you made a mistake, do what you can to correct it. And if you don't finish everything today, tomorrow is another fresh new start.

TODAY

I'll see all the possibilities.

317

November 13

*"The World's Most Exclusive Club—
Lifetime Member"*

—Sweatshirt saying

If only it were that easy. If only we could pull on a sweatshirt and suddenly be a "lifetime member" of "the world's most exclusive club." (Maybe that's why we wear clothes and shoes with designer labels.) Are you part of a group? If yes, what brought you together? If you're not part of a group, is there one you'd like to join or start?

I'll list my three favorite things to do. Is there anyone I know who likes the same things?

November 14

"You are never given a wish without also being given the power to make it true."

—Richard Bach

What do you want to be? Where do you want to go? Who do you want to meet? You probably have some idea of the life ahead of you. Perhaps some of your ideas are crazy fantasies, while others are serious and well-thought-out life plans. Other people may have opinions, but only you can decide your future. For now, let your imagination soar. Who knows where it will take you?

TODAY

I'll dream big.

November 15

"Nobody notices what I do until I don't do it."

—Saying on a wall sign

"**I**t's true," Chris sighs. "When I get things right, I'm invisible. But when I goof up, my parents notice everything." Most parents mean well. They think it's their job to point out your faults. They forget that praise is important, too. What can you do to remind your parents? Ask them for a compliment. Give them one (maybe they'll get the message). Or follow Mark Twain's advice: "If you can't get a compliment any other way, pay yourself one."

I'll give myself a compliment.

November
16

"Use wisely your power of choice."

—Og Mandino

Freedom of choice is one of our most important rights, but it's also a responsibility. Every choice has a consequence. That's why we need to be careful about the choices we make, big and small. As you're exercising your right to choose, let these words from the Buddhist *Dhammapada* guide you: "Why do what you will regret? Why bring tears upon yourself? Do only what you do not regret, and fill yourself with joy."

TODAY

I'll make a careful choice.

November
17

"Sometimes it's other people's lack of faith in you that gives you the something extra needed to help you reach your goal."

—David Brenner

Has anyone ever told you that you couldn't do something? That there was no way you could finish a particular project or reach a certain goal? How did that make you feel? Perhaps it made you want to try even harder. You wanted to succeed, just to prove you could do it. Sometimes you need encouragement to finish a task. And sometimes negative comments push you to do your best.

TODEY

I'll work toward my goals, no matter what other people say.

November 18

*"The key is not the 'will to win'...
everybody has that. It is the will to prepare
to win that is important."*

—Bobby Knight

We see winners at their winning moments—the chess champions, skating champions, and stars accepting their awards. What we don't see are the years of preparation leading up to those moments. Marilyn vos Savant says, "A few people will be at the right place at the right time by luck, but most people win by building the right place themselves and spending a heck of a lot of time there."

TODAY

I'll prepare to win.

November 19

"A problem is a chance for you to do your best."

—Duke Ellington

Rebecca Brown was bugged about something. Her town had a great baseball team, but it didn't have a library. Rebecca believed that books were as important as baseball. So she made speeches, collected signatures, and wrote newspaper articles. She and her Girl Scout troop got grant money to spend on books. Other people started listening to Rebecca. Today her town—Boyertown, Pennsylvania—has a real library.

TODAY

I'll see a problem as an
opportunity, not an obstacle.

November 20

"People need joy quite as much as clothing. Some of them need it far more."

—Margaret Collier Graham

The basic necessities of life include food, water, and shelter. Those are the things you need to survive. But you need much more to really live. Imagine life without love, friendship, and compassion—without happiness, hope, and joy. All are vital to your emotional health. Are your emotional needs being met?

I'll take care of
my emotional health.

325

November
21

"A ship in port is safe, but that's not what ships are built for."

—Grace Hopper

Dani is a gifted basketball player, the star of her school team. One day a coach from another school comes to see her. He is starting a new program especially for athletes. Would Dani like to join? It would be the best girls' basketball team in the district. Dani thinks about being part of a great team. She also thinks about no longer being the star of her own team. She decides not to join. It's too much of a risk.

TODAY

I'll accept that opportunity and risk go together.

November
22

"When I am attacked by gloomy thoughts, nothing helps me so much as running to my books."

—Michel Eyquem de Montaigne

There are days when you can't get in a good mood, no matter how hard you try. Not even your friends can cheer you up. Clouds hang over your head. You just want to be alone. So you reach for the headphones and your favorite record. Or you curl up under a blanket with your old Teddy bear and a book.

TODAY

I'll know what to do if I get the blues. I can take care of myself.

November
23

"Do not let what you cannot do interfere with what you can do."

—John Wooden

So you can't sing, or your drawing skills are nonexistent. Or you tried cooking dinner last night and you're still scraping it off the stove. Don't be so hard on yourself. Think of the things you can do. Work on the talents you have. Remember that some take longer to develop than others, and don't give up. Start with these words from St. Francis de Sales: "Have patience with all things, but first of all with yourself."

I'll be patient with myself.

November
24

"You are here for a purpose. There is not a duplicate of you in the whole wide world; there never has been, there never will be. You were brought here now to fill a certain need."

—Lou Austin

What is your purpose? What need can you fill? Why are you here? These are big questions, and people may tell you it's too soon to ask them. Ask anyway. Ask your friends and family. Ask your teachers, minister, or rabbi. You will learn much about yourself if you're not afraid to ask big questions.

TODAY

I'll ask a big question.

November
25

"A true friend is someone who is there for you when he'd rather be anywhere else."

—Len Wein

There's more to being a good friend than eating lunch together and talking on the phone. There's more to it than going to the movies and hanging out on weekends. To be a good friend, you must be willing to listen. Even when you don't really feel like listening. Even when your friend has said it all before. Listen to the meaning behind the words. Is your friend in trouble? Does your friend have a problem? How can you help?

TODAY

I'll take time to really listen to a friend.

November 26

"The great secret of success is to go through life as a person who never gets used up."

—Albert Schweitzer

Angela, 14, says: "Lots of times I'll find myself with tons of stuff piled up, and I get frustrated because I know that I've got to do it all, and I realize how long it'll take... Then I've got to ask myself, 'Is this what I truly want to do? Or am I doing this because someone else wants me to, or because I'm capable of doing well? Is it important to me?'"

TODAY

I'll ask myself, "Are the things I'm doing important to me?"

November 27

"In the race for quality, there is no finish line."

—David T. Kearns

Have you ever rushed through an assignment, then had to do it over because it was sloppy or incomplete? If only you'd done it right the first time....But you've heard it all before. Either the quality of your work is important to you, or it isn't. If it isn't, then you're probably not very proud of it. And if you're not proud of your work, you may not feel very good about yourself. (You can choose to change.)

TODAY

I'll take my time and do it right.

November 28

"It is better to have loafed and lost than never to have loafed at all."

—James Thurber

What's your favorite way to loaf? Some possibilities:

1. Snoozing on the couch.
2. Watching Errol Flynn pirate movies.
3. Taking an hour-long bubble bath and getting completely wrinkled.
4. Paging through old *Garfield* cartoon books.
5. Paging through old family photo albums.
6. _____?

Pick one, then do it today. (The only things you'll lose by loafing are stress, tension, and anxiety.)

I'll loaf.

November
29

"In your own life, it's hard to know when to stop acting, because you get so wrapped up in it."

—Loretta Young

It would be great if we could all just be ourselves. But we worry that people won't like us if we are. So we act like other people— popular people. We do things we don't really want to do, and say things we don't really mean. We even pretend to believe things we don't believe. It's all an act. And if people like us that way, we keep on acting.

TODAY

I'll be myself.

November 30

> *"When I was a boy of fourteen, my father was so ignorant I could hardly stand to have the old man around. But when I got to be twenty-one, I was astonished at how much he had learned in seven years."*
>
> —Mark Twain

Did Mark Twain's father really get smarter? Maybe yours will, too. Or maybe your parents are pretty smart already, and you just haven't noticed it lately. What do you think? (P.S. Today is Mark Twain's birthday.)

TODAY

I'll try to appreciate my parents or other adults who take care of me.

December 1

"Some people don't find out what they want to be until they're 35. I knew when I was 4."

—Mariah Carey

Mariah Carey always wanted to be a singer. Today she's a star. What are your interests? What are your talents? Can you find any clues to your future in the person you are today? Try to look beyond the most obvious ones. If you're someone who likes animals, you don't have to become a veterinarian. Maybe you can work at an animal shelter.

TODAY

I'll picture my future self. What do I see me doing?

December
2

"I'll tell you what sustains you. You go back to the advice you got as a kid—do your best. Try your hardest. Work hard and get the best advice you can."

—George Bush

Presidents have advisers. These are experts in certain areas: education, the economy, and so on. If you could put together a group of your own advisers, who would they be? What would they be experts in? Answer these questions and you may be on your way to finding a mentor—an adult who works with you, guides you, answers your questions, and helps you explore future careers.

TODAY

I'll think about finding a mentor.

December
3

"When angry, count to four; when very angry, swear."

—Mark Twain

Compared to other responses to anger, swearing seems harmless. (Especially if you do it in private.) But anger itself can cause problems for you. If you are angry a lot, it can even make you sick. Sister Elizabeth Kenny faced her anger when she was a young girl. She tells this story: "As a girl my temper often got out of bounds. But one day when I became angry at a friend over some trivial matter, my mother told me, 'Elizabeth, anyone who angers you conquers you.'"

TODAY

I'll learn more about why I get angry.

338

December 4

"Take time every day to do something silly."

—Philipa Walker

If you've been too serious lately, you may need some silly practice first. Start by making faces in a mirror. Stick out your tongue, puff out your cheeks, make a fish mouth, wiggle your eyebrows....From there, you can graduate to higher forms of silliness. For ideas, check out silly videos. Possibilities: The Three Stooges, The Marx Brothers, Monty Python movies.

I'll do something silly.

December 5

"Most folks are about as happy as they make up their minds to be."

—Abraham Lincoln

You are responsible for your own feelings. This means that you can choose to be happy. And why shouldn't you? Maybe the world is a scary place. Maybe there are things about your life you'd like to change. Maybe you worry about the future. Who doesn't? You can still choose to be happy. You have the power. It's all in your mind.

TODAY

I'll make up my mind to be happy.

December
6

"I believe that true identity is found in creative activity springing from within. It is found when one loses oneself."

—Anne Morrow Lindbergh

Cary spends hours composing music on his keyboard. When Lara dances, the world disappears. Zach has been inventing things since he was five years old. Is there something you lose yourself in? When do you feel most creative, most alive, most you?

I'll spend time with my creative self.

December
7

"If you constantly think of illness, you eventually become ill; if you believe yourself to be beautiful, you become so."

—Shakti Gawain

Over 2,000 years ago, the Buddha taught, "We are what we think...With our thoughts we make our world." In our own time, Dr. Norman Vincent Peale said, "Change your thoughts and you change your world." Other beliefs have come and gone with the changing centuries. But wise men and women have always believed in the power of positive thinking.

TODAY

I'll start changing my thoughts to make a better world for myself.

December
8

"Not to know is bad. Not to want to know is worse."

—West African proverb

What happens when you don't know the answer to a question? Do you forget about it, or find out about it? You may have heard the saying, "Ignorance is bliss." Don't believe it. Instead, ask questions. Be curious. Have an inquiring mind. And never give up. If you really want to know something, keep searching for the answer. If other people don't know it, and you can't find it in books, you may have to discover it for yourself.

I'll be a curious cat.

December
9

"Be content to make one difference in one other person's life. That's enough."

—Thom Buescher

Many young people today are choosing to be socially active. Some are working for the environment, endangered species, the homeless—big stuff. Others are working on smaller, more personal projects. Only you can decide what's right for you. If you decide to organize your whole town to start recycling, that's great. If you decide to help one neighbor bundle up old newspapers, that's great, too.

TODAY

I'll make a difference in someone else's life.

December 10

"It wasn't raining when Noah built the ark."

—Howard Ruff

Why did Noah build the ark? Because he had faith. He believed that God would send the flood. He trusted that the ark would keep him and his family safe. What do you have faith in? God? Yourself? Other people? Your abilities? Samuel Butler once said, "You can do very little with faith, but you can do nothing without it." What do you think he meant?

I'll have faith.

December
11

"I think self-awareness is probably the most important thing towards being a champion."

—Billie Jean King

Strength is important to an athlete. Curiosity is important to a reporter. A love of performing is important to an actor. Whatever you decide to do with your life, you'll need to develop specific talents. But one thing all champions need is self-awareness—a clear mental picture of who they are, what they can do, and what's important to them. Take time to get to know yourself. Find out what kind of person you are.

TODAY

I'll get to know myself better.

December 12

"Fate chooses our relatives, we choose our friends."

—Jacques DeLille

Most of us are stuck with the families we're born into. This can be great or not so great. And it's not unusual for kids to sometimes wish they had been born into different families. (Have you ever wanted to be one of the Cosbys? The Cleavers? The Simpsons?) Are you mostly happy with your family, or mostly unhappy? If you're mostly unhappy, find someone to talk to.

TODAY

I'll think of three things I really like about my family.

347

December
13

"My favorite thing is to go where I've never been."

—Diane Arbus

Have you ever traveled to a foreign country? Do you remember what it was like to hear the language, read street signs, and watch TV? How did you feel—excited? anxious? happy? curious? confused? Experiences like these help us grow. But even if you haven't traveled, you can still go places you've never been. Check out a video. Listen to a language lesson on audio cassette. Read a book. You can go anywhere in your mind.

TODAY

I'll list three countries I'd like to visit someday.

December
14

"Slow down so you can go faster."

—Ken Blanchard

Jill races through her math worksheet and gets four wrong. Theo hurries to finish a book report and forgets to check his work. Lin speeds through her spelling homework and fails a pop quiz. Going too fast can cause problems. As someone once said, "If you don't have time to do it right, when will you have time to do it over?"

I'll take time to do things right.

December 15

"I will love you no matter what. I will love you if you are stupid, if you slip and fall on your face, if you do the wrong thing, if you make mistakes, if you behave like a human being—I will love you no matter."

—Leo Buscaglia

Leo Buscaglia is talking about unconditional love. This is the kind of love most parents feel for their children. It is the kind of love some friends feel for each other. This kind of love does not keep score. It just...is.

TODAY

I'll be grateful for the unconditional love in my life.

December 16

"Being under stress is like being inside a ball of rubber bands."

—Earl Hipp

For many people, the holidays are very stressful. How can you lessen your stress? Start with these basic self-care skills:

- Exercise. Pick an activity you enjoy: walking, swimming, running.
- Eat sensibly. Cut out caffeine. (Many soft drinks contain caffeine. Read the labels.)
- Practice relaxing. Watch TV, take a nap, call a friend, read a book.

TODAY

I'll try at least one of these self-care skills.

December 17

"I've come to have a very strong belief in my instincts."

—Jill Eikenberry

Who's the best person to turn to when you've got a tough decision to make? You. Who will give you the best advice when you're faced with a new situation? You again. Other people may be quick to give advice, but if the advice doesn't work out they're also quick to blame you for not doing exactly what they said. You are responsible for yourself. Trust yourself.

TODAY

I'll trust myself.

352

December 18

"I've learned that nobody's perfect, and I don't expect myself to be perfect anymore."

—Carly Simon

The Roman poet Virgil said it simply: "We cannot do all things." If you try to do everything, you won't do anything well. If you strive to be perfect, you will fail. Accept your limits and work within them. You will excel in some areas and not in others. You will choose to work harder on the ones you care most about. You will learn and change and grow.

I won't even try to be perfect.

December
19

"Your expression is the most important thing you can wear."

—Sid Ascher

Out of all the clothes in your closet, what's your favorite outfit? Whatever you choose will look even better with a smile. It sounds corny, but try it. You'll see the difference in how people talk to you and treat you.

**I'll smile more
and see what happens.**

December 20

"Having it all doesn't necessarily mean having it all at once."

—Stephanie Luetkehans

Commercials push you to buy or do this or look like that. Sometimes it's enough to drive you crazy. But you know you can't have everything at once. Look on the positive side and see what you do have. And don't just count your material possessions. Count the things that are more important: friendship, health, education, family, self-worth, love. See how rich you are?

TODAY

I'll feel good about all the non-material things I have.

December 21

"Success has nothing to do with what you gain in life or accomplish for yourself. It's what you do for others."

—Danny Thomas

Throughout your life, you've been pretty busy looking out for yourself. You've pursued your own interests and done things you've wanted to do. Now, how about looking out for someone else? You have time to help a younger brother or sister with homework. Or you can volunteer to cook dinner. Does a neighbor need help in any way? Is the park looking for a clean-up crew? Don't just think about it. Do it.

I'll spend part of the day doing something for somebody else.

December
22

"I'm learning more and more that love plus attachment equals pain."

—Lisa Bonet

When you love someone, you take a risk. And when you get so attached that you can't bear to be apart, you risk losing yourself. You know couples who are always together. They don't have lives of their own. They finish each others' sentences and think each others' thoughts. Some people think this must be true love. But true love leaves room for independence. It lets people be themselves. It respects individual wants and needs.

TODAY

I'll love without losing myself.

December 23

"One day at a time! It's a wholesome rhyme; a good one to live by, a day at a time."

—Helen Hunt Jackson

In growing up, there are no shortcuts. You have to be 12 years old before you can be 13 or 16 or 20. You have to finish middle school before you can start high school. You have to take the months and years in order, with no skipping or cheating. So does everyone else. In a way, it's nice to know that a day is a day no matter who you are.

I'll just think of today.

December
24

"How beautiful it is to do nothing, and then rest afterward."

—Proverb

WHAT? Do nothing in the middle of the holidays? Isn't that impossible? Not for you—remember, you're a positive thinker. Go ahead and help out around the house. Make your own preparations, too. Then take a long bath or go to bed an hour early. Put this at the top of your Things-To-Do list. Ashleigh Brilliant says, "Sometimes the most urgent and vital thing you can possibly do is take a complete rest."

TODAY

I'll rest.

359

December
25

"Today I will believe that as I give to the world, the world will give to me."

—Earnie Larsen

Give yourself a push with three more giving sayings:

- Kahlil Gibran: "You give but little when you give of your possessions. It is when you give of yourself that you truly give."
- Eleanor Roosevelt: "Think as little as possible about yourself and as much as possible about other people....Put a good deal of thought into the happiness that you are able to give."
- Madeline Bridges: "Give to the world the best you have, and the best will come back to you."

TODAY

I'll give of myself.

December
26

"Not everything that is faced can be changed. But nothing can be changed until it is faced."

—James Baldwin

The New Year is just around the corner. How would you like it to be different from all the other years of your life? What truth, problem, or habit can you face? Can you make a change, large or small, that will ripple down the year like a pebble falling in a pond?

TODAY

I'll make a change.

December
27

"Learn day by day to broaden your horizons."

—Ethel Barrymore

J ust for fun, learn something new today. Pick up a book on a subject you know nothing about. Turn the TV to a cable program on science, politics, or the arts. Read an article in a magazine you've never looked at before. Ask a question. Add to the wonderful person you already are.

I'll learn something new.

December
28

"You are God's work of art."

—St. Paul

Is your nose too big? Are your eyes too small? Would you like to be taller, shorter, richer, smarter? It's so easy to criticize ourselves. We can always find things we don't like about our looks, talents, abilities, personality, family, friends—all the circumstances of our lives. If we could make ourselves over, we'd do a much better job. (Or would we?)

TODAY

**I'll be happy with myself,
just the way I am, from head to toe,
inside and out.**

December
29

"Follow your dreams."

—Wil Wheaton

If you began this year by writing down your dreams (see page 1), you may want to look at them now. How many came true? How many were forgotten? If you didn't begin this year by writing down your dreams, there's always next year....Or just think about them today. Daydream your favorite. Imagine yourself as the star of your dream. Don't limit yourself; in your dreams, you can do and be anything.

I'll dream.

December
30

"Write it in your heart that every day is the best day in the year."

—Ralph Waldo Emerson

I t's almost New Year's Day. For many people, this means pressure. They promise to change their lives. They write a long list of resolutions. Then they try to do everything on one day. And when they fail at one resolution, they give up on all the rest. This New Year, don't make any resolutions. Just treat tomorrow as another day. Then make the most of it in your own way.

I'll welcome the best day of my life.

December
31

"What we call the beginning is often the end. And to make an end is to make a beginning. The end is where we start from."

—T.S. Eliot

A book has a beginning and an end. A year has a beginning and an end. Now that you have come to the end of this book, you may want to begin it again. Now that you have come to the end of the year, it's time for a new beginning. Be happy, be peaceful, be yourself, love and respect yourself, don't try to be perfect, and reach out to others. Start there.

TODAY

I begin.

Subject Index

People
(and others)
Index

Information has been adapted or excerpted from the following Free Spirit materials for the entries noted, with permission of the publisher: *Bringing Out the Best: A Resource Guide for Parents of Young Gifted Children* by Jacqulyn Saunders with Pamela Espeland (April 28); *Dreams Can Help: A Journal Guide to Understanding Your Dreams and Making Them Work for You* by Jonni Kincher (January 24, March 12); *Fighting Invisible Tigers: A Stress Management Guide for Teens* by Earl Hipp (March 31, April 18, June 6, June 11, December 16); *Free Spirit: News & Views on Growing Up*: Vol. 1 No. 5 (November 26); Vol. 3 No. 2 (November 9); Vol. 3 No. 4 (May 1); Vol. 4 No. 2 (September 1, December 2); Vol. 4 No. 3 (April 19, May 26, July 23, August 24, October 13); Vol. 4 No. 4 (August 19, September 9); *How To Help Your Child with Homework: Every Caring Parent's Guide to Encouraging Good Study Habits and Ending the Homework Wars* by Marguerite Radencich and Jeanne Shay Schumm (September 17); *It's All In Your Head: A Guide to Understanding Your Brain and Boosting Your Brain Power* by Susan L. Barrett (April 13); *The Kid's Guide to Social Action: How to Solve the Social Problems You Choose— and Turn Creative Thinking into Positive Action* by Barbara A. Lewis (January 5, February 19, November 10); *Kidstories: Biographies of 20 Young People You'd Like to Know* by James Delisle (May 7); *Perfectionism: What's Bad About Being Too Good?* by Miriam Adderholdt-Elliott (January 20, February 20, June 15, August 6, September 19, September 25); *Psychology for Kids: 40 Fun Tests That Help You Learn About Yourself* by Jonni Kincher (January 3, July 11, October 27); *Stick Up For Yourself! Every Kid's Guide to Personal Power and Positive Self-Esteem* by Gershen Kaufman and Lev Raphael (January 8, February 21, March 28, April 1-2, August 20, September 4, November 8); *The Survival Guide for Kids with LD (Learning Differences)* by Gary Fisher and Rhoda Cummings (July 6); *The Survival Guide for Parents of Gifted Kids: How to Understand, Live With, and Stick Up for Your Gifted Child* by Sally Yahnke Walker (April 27); *You and Stress: A Survival Guide for Adolescence* by Gail C. Roberts and Lorraine Guttormson (September 22).